Where to See Wildlife
in California

by Tom Taber

ISBN: 0-9609170-1-2

PHOTO CREDITS:

California State Department of Fish and Game: pages 2, 26, 33, 35, 50, 52, 60, 64, 79, 127, 130
California State Department of Parks and Recreation: pages 6, 12, 69, 89, 125, 126.
California Academy of Sciences: pages 25, 43, 45, 92, 97.
United States Fish and Wildlife Service: pages 29, 93.
Richard Mattison: page 77.
Seattle Aquarium: page 80.
Simone Morton Dangles: page 113.
Regina Taber: page 121.
Tom Taber: pages 21, 36, 49, 56, 82, 90, 116.
Marc Webber: front cover.

THE OAK VALLEY PRESS
228 Virginia Ave.,
San Mateo, CA 94402

Contents:

WILDLIFE LOCATIONS:

1 Agate Beach County Park
2 Año Nuevo State Reserve
3 Anza Borrega Desert State Park
4 Audubon Canyon Ranch
5 Bodega Bay
6 Bodega Head
7 Bolinas
8 Bolsa Chica Ecological Reserve
9 Cabrillo Museum
10 Cabrillo National Monument
11 California Bighorn Sheep
Zoological Area
12 California Marine Mammal
Center
13 Carmel River State Beach
14 Carpinteria State Beach
15 Channel Islands National Park
16 Cucamonga Wilderness
17 Death Valley National
Monument
18 Eagle Lake
19 Farallon Islands

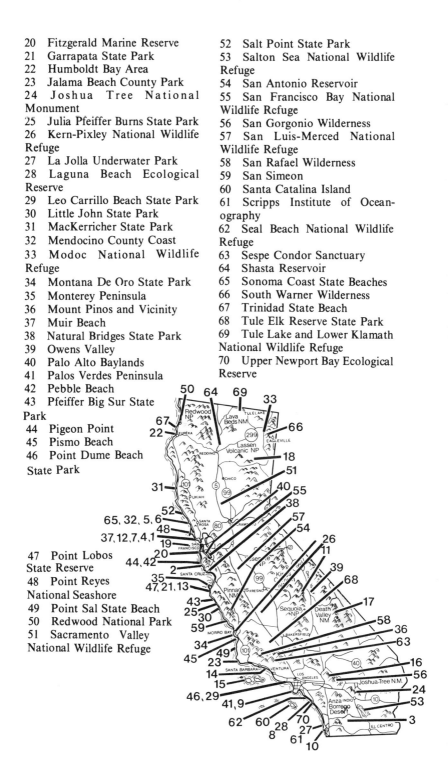

INTRODUCTION:
An Abundance of Life

THERE IS NO more thrilling and inspiring sight than that of wildlife living free. On visits to the wild and natural places of California there is often the expectation of seeing wild animals--even a fleeting glimpse--that will be the highlight of the trip.

It may come as a surprise even to natives of the Golden State that we are second only to Alaska in our abundance and diversity of wildlife. The diversity of California, with its mountains and valleys, deserts and rainforests, palm trees and glaciers, and all manner of seashore, islands, marshes, and rivers, can scarcely be matched anywhere else in the world. Our wildlife heritage includes seals, sea lions, sea otters, whales, bighorn sheep, elk, deer, cougars, endless varieties of birdlife--including eagles and condors-- and that's just to scratch the surface.

This wealth of natural beauty and ecological diversity is even more remarkable when you consider that much of it nearly vanished in this century. Gray whales, sea otters, brown pelicans, tule elk, elephant seals, bald eagles, and fur seals have made astounding comebacks from the edge of extinction because people cared enough to do something to save them. People changed their thinking about wildlife, wilderness, and our relationship with nature; and a conservation ethic took hold in California that has spread through much of the world. We showed that a rapidly growing human population can coexist with other species; and that we can respect and appreciate other life forms for their beauty, their personal integrity, and their place in the community of life.

Unfortunately, the picture is not all bright. Bighorn sheep are only now starting to show signs of recovery, and the California condor, North America's largest bird, is now nearly extinct. There are many threats to wildlife that may continue to increase, including toxic wastes, pesticides, oil spills, and loss of habitat. There is much to be done, and a good place to start is to take a look at what we have that is worth protecting.

I am firmly convinced that the best way to foster an ecological awareness is to encourage people to visit our mountains, deserts, forests, wetlands, and seashores. There are no more passionate defenders of wildlife than those who have personal experiences in the wild. People who have seen sea otters frolic in the kelp beds are their best allies; those who have witnessed whales breaching and spouting on their journey down the coast are their most willing defenders. It is my hope that this book will help to build a constituency for wildlife and for their natural habitats.

My main focus is wildlife you are likely to see in specific places. There is no way to include every place where all wild animals can be found, and this is especially true of birds, which are found in diversity and abundance throughout the state. Instead, I have included the most impressive and accessible displays of wildlife. Elephant seals, for example, are always found at Año Nuevo in winter. Other species, such as elk, may require a little more patience; and some animals, such as bighorn sheep, are seen only in the rugged and remote wildernesses. I give less emphasis to coyotes, montain lions, bobcats, and many others that are found over large areas, and not concentrated where they may be readily seen.

The best way to see wildlife is to walk softly and keep your eyes and ears alert and attuned to your surroundings. California's wildlands are not zoos, and the animals that live there must be encountered on their own terms -- which is often when you least expect it. Always travel with respect in natural places, and remember that you· are in someone's home.

Bald Eagles

NO MATTER HOW many pictures you have seen, the sight of bald eagles soaring wild and free will form a lasting impression. Their features are bold, their colors are striking in combination, and they soar with a grace and majesty befitting a national symbol. More than just beautiful, bald eagles are perhaps the most truly magnificent birds in the world.

Not long ago the pesticide DDT permeated the eagles' food chain and made their eggs too weak to hatch. Unrestricted pesticide use, coupled with a loss of habitat and illegal shooting, left little reason for hope for bald eagles in California. But conservationists did not give up hope, and after years of work their efforts have begun to pay off. The banning of DDT, and the control of other pesticides, the protection of key habitat, captive breeding, and transplant from Alaska, offers the possibility that they will be a common sight for future generations in this state. As for now, they are still a rare sight in California, and the struggle to protect them is not over.

Easily identified by brownish-black bodies, white heads and tails, and large yellow-hooked bills, bald eagles range through much of the state in winter, and are most commonly seen near large streams, reservoirs, and lakes. They court in mid-winter and lay eggs

WHERE TO SEE BALD EAGLES:

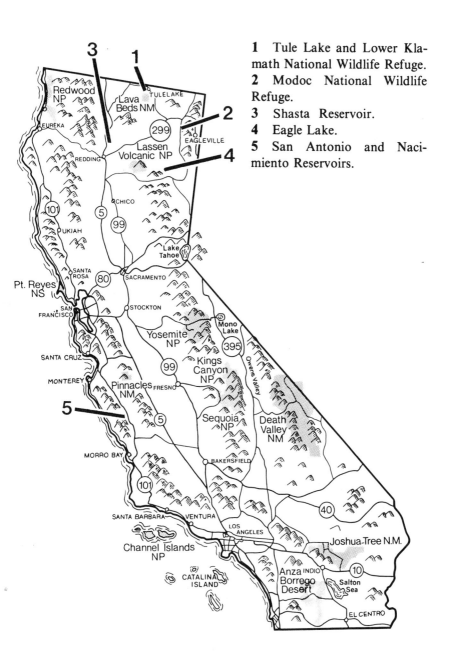

1 Tule Lake and Lower Klamath National Wildlife Refuge.
2 Modoc National Wildlife Refuge.
3 Shasta Reservoir.
4 Eagle Lake.
5 San Antonio and Nacimiento Reservoirs.

Bald eagles are magnificent, but their voices are surprisingly weak. Listen for a thin, chittering "Kleek-kik-ik-ik-ik," or a lower "kak-kak-kak."

from mid-February to April. Their nests are easily identified large platforms of sticks in trees. Eagles mate for life, both parents helping to care for the young, which leave the nests in eight to ten weeks. Their eight-foot wingspan allows them to traverse the sky with ease in search of fish, waterfowl, carrion, and other prey. They usually prefer fish -- salmon in particular -- but will go after waterfowl when fish is less available. Their vision is so acute they can see small prey three miles away.

Eagles come down from Alaska and Canada with the storms of late fall and early winter, and may be seen near lakes and reservoirs throughout the state. In most of the state they are only occasionally seen, but in a few places they are regular visitors. Here are some of the best places to look for bald eagles in California:

Tule Lake and Lower Klamath National Wildlife Refuge

TO GET THERE... from the town of Tulelake take East-West Road five miles west and turn south on Hill Road to refuge headquarters. From the Central Valley, the San Francisco Area, and Southern California, take Highway 5 north past Mount Shasta, turn northeast on Highway 97, and east on Highway 161.

The Klamath Basin area is the most likely place in the state to see bald eagles. More than 500 of the birds winter here, making it the largest concentration in the country south of Alaska. They feed on the abundance of waterfowl, which helps make this one of the most ideal bald eagle habitats in California. Each morning, before sunrise, bald eagles can be seen on the frozen lakes feeding on crippled and dead waterfowl. They spend the rest of the day perching in nearby trees, and roost for the night in the forested mountains surrounding the basin. They usually start arriving about mid-November and are most abundant in late December and January. You can see them from the self-guided auto tour routes.

Be sure to stop at refuge headquarters, or call, for current viewing information: Refuge Manager, U.S. Fish and Wildlife Service, Route 1, Box 74, Tulelake, CA 96134; (916) 667-2231.

See map on pages 38 and 39.

Modoc National Wildlife Refuge
TO GET THERE... take Highway 395 south from Alturas, turn east on County Road 56, and south on County Road 115. It's in Modoc County.

This 6,016-acre refuge for waterfowl is also an occasional han-

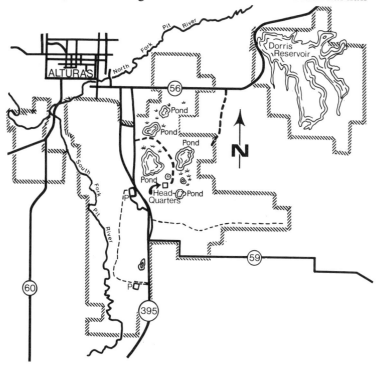

gout for bald eagles, especially from December to February. For current information, contact: Modoc National Wildlife Refuge, P.O. Box 1610, Alturas, CA 96101; (916) 233-3572.

Shasta Reservoir

TO GET THERE... it's just north of Redding on Highway 5, in Shasta County.

Eighteen bald eagles were recently sighted here in early winter, where they feed on waterfowl and fish. Lakeside campsites are provided. For more information, contact: Shasta Cascade Wonderland Association, P.O. Box 1988, Redding, CA 96099; (916) 243-2643.

Eagle Lake

TO GET THERE... take Highway 139 or A-1 county road north from Susanville, in Lassen County.

This relatively large lake is the wintering home of at least 43 bald eagles. This beautiful body of water is uncrowded all year and has Forest Service Campgrounds nearby. For more information, contact: Lassen National Forest, 707 Nevada Street, Susanville, CA 96130; (916) 257-2151.

San Antonio Reservoir

TO GET THERE... from Highway 101 take county road G-18 west from Bradley. It's in southern Monterey County.

A recent bird count tallied 36 bald eagles thriving here and at nearby Nacimiento Reservoir. Camping is allowed at both lakes. For more information, contact: U.S. Fish and Wildlife Service, (916) 440-2202.

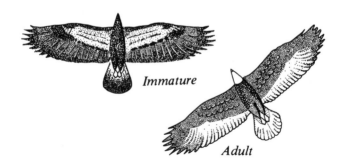

Immature

Adult

Birds

... sea birds, raptors, shore birds, marsh birds, and waterfowl.

THE GOLDEN STATE has such an abundance and diversity of birdlife, that it would be hopeless to try to include every place to see them in this book. For this reason I include only some of the best places to see the most extraordinary displays of birds. The best way to learn more about birding in your area is in the company of other birders, who will be glad to share their expertise. There are many groups to join, perhaps the best being the Audubon Society, which has chapters throughout the state. It is also helpful to have a good pair of binoculars and a field guide. Two of the best are: *A Field Guide to Western Birds* (Peterson, Houghton Mifflin Co., 1980), *The Audubon Society Field Guide to North American Birds* (Alfred A. Knopf, 1977); and *Birds of North America* (Golden Press, 1966).

The following locations are arranged geographically, from south to north:

Salton Sea National Wildlife Refuge
TO GET THERE... from El Centro take Route 86 north to Brawley, turn north on Highway 111 and left on Sinclair Road to the refuge.

Wintering concentrations of waterfowl help to make this 35,484-acre preserve one of Southern California's best birding places. January through March is the best time to see great concentra-

WHERE TO SEE BIRDS:

1 Salton Sea National Wildlife Refuge.
2 Bolsa Chica Ecological Reserve.
3 Seal Beach National Wildlife Refuge.
4 Upper Newport Bay Ecological Reserve.
5 Channel Islands National Park.
6 Kern-Pixley National Wildlife Refuge.
7 Morro Bay.
8 Point Lobos State Reserve.
9 San Luis-Merced National Wildlife Refuge.
10 San Francisco Bay National Wildlife Refuge.
11 Palo Alto Baylands.
12 Farallon Islands National Wildlife Refuge.
13 Audubon Canyon Ranch.
14 Point Reyes National Seashore.
15 Sacramento Valley National Wildlife Refuge.
16 Humboldt Bay National Wildlife Refuge.
17 Modoc National Wildlife Refuge.
18 Tule Lake and Lower Klamath National Wildlife Refuge.

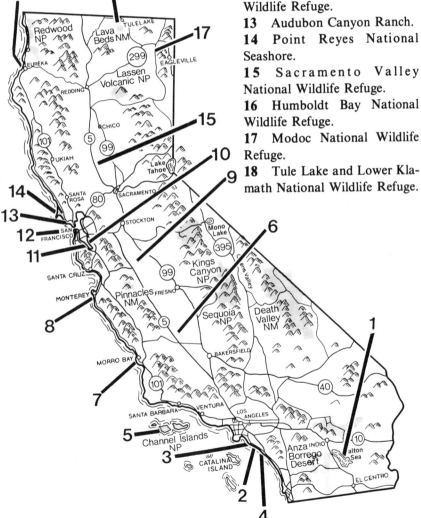

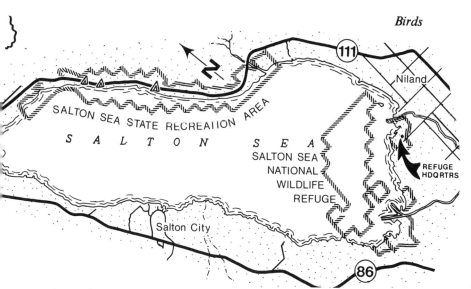

tions of shorebirds, ducks, and geese. Late spring and summer is the time to see woodstorks, and blue-footed and brown boobies. This area also has the greatest number of doves in the west. Other birds to look for include rough-winged and bank swallows, Scotts orioles, orange-crowned and yellow-rumped warblers, burrowing owls, long-billed dowitchers, redstarts, mountain plovers, and long-billed marsh wrens.

This refuge is on the shores and waters of the Salton Sea, which covers 375 square miles and has 115 miles of shoreline. It was formed in 1905 when the Colorado River broke through a channel and flowed downhill to this basin, which was 228 feet below sea level. The preserve has few formal trails, though the dikes are good for walking. Camping is at the Salton Sea State Receation Area. For more information, contact: Salton Sea National Wildlife Refuge, P.O. Box 247, Calipatria, CA 92233; (619) 348-2323.

Bolsa Chica Ecological Reserve
TO GET THERE... from the San Diego Freeway (Highway 405) drive west on Golden West Street, and turn north on Highway 1. It's across the highway from Bolsa Chica State Park.

As many as seven thousand resident and migratory waterfowl are seen here at a time during the winter months. There is a one-mile nature trail.

Seal Beach National Wildlife Refuge
TO GET THERE... in Orange County, it is just northwest of Huntington Beach on Highway 1.

This 977-acre preserve, in the U.S. Naval Weapons Station, sets aside the largest salt marsh in Southern California. Shore and marsh birds are abundant, and can be seen from the Coast Highway near Surfside, and from Edinger Avenue in Huntington Beach.

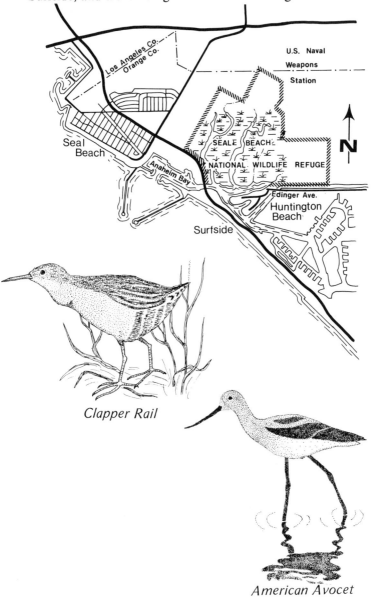

Clapper Rail

American Avocet

Upper Newport Bay Ecological Reserve

TO GET THERE... in Orange County, it's inland from the town of Newport Beach, on Highway 1.

This 752-acre salt marsh is one of Southern California's most important coastal wetlands. Herons and egrets are among the shore and marsh birds seen from self-guided nature trails. Once a month the Friends of Newport Bay provide two-hour guided tours of the reserve. For more information, call Friends of Newport Bay: (714) 646-8009.

The protection of these remaining wetlands is vital. In this century California has lost two-thirds of its coastal marshes, and Southern California--below Point Conception--has saved only 22 per cent of its original wetlands. These salt marshes and shallow coastal waters form one of the world's most productive and important sources of nutrients for the food chain.

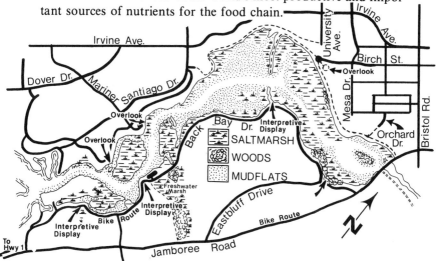

Channel Islands National Park

TO GET THERE... commercial passenger service is available from several Southern California ports. Additional information is mentioned below.

The urbanized Southern California coast has its salvation in the wild and rugged Channel Islands anchored offshore. Just a few dozen miles from the state's most populous metropolitan area, sea and shore birds, as well as seals, sea lions, and other marine life, are thriving in their natural habitat. To protect the islands' fragile ecology, access is limited.

This park is composed of five islands--all worth exploring. The most popular time to go is summer, when days are long, though some days are foggy. Spring and fall offer more solitude, and some of the best weather, and even winter makes way for some mild and sunny days between storms.

Year-round boat trips are provided by: Island Packers, 1695 Anchors Way Drive, Ventura, CA 93003; (805) 642-1393. This concessionaire is the only operation running on a regular basis. They make an effort to pass by areas of wildlife interest for day users and island campers. It is best to phone two weeks ahead for reservations. For more information, contact: Channel Islands National Park, 1901 Spinnaker Drive, Ventura, CA 93001; (805) 644-8262.

ANACAPA ISLAND: These chunks of rock thrust out of the ocean, offering the only nesting site for the endangered brown pelicans on the west coast of the United States. Look for their large stick platform nests on West Anacapa between May and August, when most females lay and hatch three or four eggs. After eight to ten weeks the young accompany their parents on fishing trips up and down the California coast. Most of the state's pelicans are born farther south, on the small rocky islands off the Baja California coast.

Pelicans feed by folding their wings and plummeting vertically into the water after fish. These wonderful, grayish-brown birds were headed for extinction in the 1960's because concentrations of the pesticide DDT made their eggs too fragile to hatch. In 1970, out of 442 nesting attempts on this island, only one egg hatched. Fortunately, this pesticide was banned in 1971, and pelicans are making a steady comeback, though they are still on the endangered species list. Other birds you may see here include western gulls, scoter ducks, and

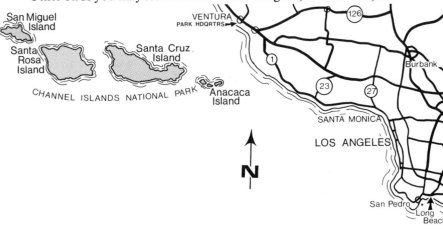

Brown pelican in winter plumage. Feeding mainly on anchovies, these birds are threatened by overfishing by humans.

Arch Rock, near the East Anacapa landing, is a popular perch for pelicans, cormorants, and other birds.

black oystercatchers. California sea lions and harbor seals are also common. Campers must register at park headquarters and must bring their own fuel, water, and shelter. Be prepared to carry your provisions up 153 steps to the island's plateau. Camping, which requires the written permission of the park superintendent, is only allowed on the east island. West Anacapa is protected as a brown pelican rookery.

SAN MIGUEL ISLAND: The western-most of the Channel Islands, San Miguel has three of Southern California's five major sea bird colonies. Auklets, cormorants, gulls, guillemots, and snowy plovers nest here. Six species of seals and sea lions come ashore, including elephant seals. The largest land mammal is the endangered San Miguel Island fox.

Access to this island is limited to Cuyler Harbor, and camping and day use are allowed by permit from park headquarters.

SANTA BARBARA ISLAND: This 640-acre lonely outpost of land is a wildlife-lovers' paradise. Western gulls and cormorants nest on the island's precipitous palisades; and even at 38 miles from San Pedro Harbor, land birds, such as burrowing owls, American kestrels, meadowlarks, and horned larks are seen. Seals and sea lions are also a common sight.

Camping is allowed near the ranger's quarters by permit from park headquarters. Bring food, water, fuel, and shelter; and don't forget binoculars.

SANTA CRUZ ISLAND: The largest of the Channel Islands, Santa Cruz is administered by the Nature Conservancy, a non-profit conservation organization that offers naturalist-led outings and interpretive programs. For more information, contact: The Nature Conservancy, Santa Cruz Island Project, 735 State Street, Suite 201, Santa Barbara, CA 93101; (805) 962-9111.

Kern-Pixley National Wildlife Refuge
TO GET THERE... take Highway 99 north from Bakersfield and take the first Delano exit. Turn left (west) on Garces Avenue, which ends at refuge headquarters.

When California was wild there was a vast body of water — in

Glaucous-Winged Gull

fact, the largest freshwater lake west of the Mississippi — in the southern Central Valley. It was gradually diked, pumped, and filled, and eventually entirely evaporated in the dry, hot climate.

Today a small remnant of these ancient wetlands has been restored at this 15,000-acre wildlife refuge; and a surprising amount of migratory waterfowl still winter here. During wet years you will find hundreds of thousands of ducks and geese, egrets, eared and piedbilled grebes, and shorebirds such as yellowlegs, long-billed curlews, dowitchers, avocets, stilts, and sandpipers. Birding can be pretty slim during dry years. March is a good month to visit, when large numbers of Canadian snow geese stop to feed. Other animals you might see include blunt-nosed leopard lizards and San Joaquin kit foxes — both endangered species -- and raccoons, jackrabbits, and coyotes.

For more information, contact: Kern-Pixley National Wildlife Refuge, P.O. Box 219, Delano, CA 93215; (805) 725-2767.

Morro Bay
TO GET THERE... In San Luis Obispo County, Morro Rock and Morro Bay State Park are in the town of Morro Bay.

Peregrine falcons, one of the most endangered species, nest on Morro Rock, now an ecological reserve with restricted public access. Nesting begins in early February, producing two to four eggs usually in April. In 28 to 31 days the chicks hatch and are closely attended by both parents. Peregrines mate for life, and return each year to the same nest site. They are also one of the world's fastest flying predatory birds, sometimes reaching 175 miles per hour while diving after small birds -- their main diet. They have a wingspan of about three feet and are seen as grayish hawk-like birds. Females are browner than males.

Peregrines were nearly wiped out by reproductive failure due to the pesticide DDT, which caused calcium deficiencies. In 1970 there were fewer than ten nesting pairs in California. Fortunately, there has been an increase in reproductive success since the pesticide was banned in 1971.

Peregrines started nesting at Morro Rock in the spring of 1967, and their preservation has been an uphill struggle ever since. In 1971 climbers scaled the cliff at night and stole two chicks from the nest, and since then the State Department of Fish and Game has posted guards on top of the rock for the three-month nesting period. In 1977 a male peregrine was struck in flight by a gunshot. The main threat, however, is still pesticides. The falcons that nest here prey on migratory fish-eating birds from Central American countries where DDT continues to be used. As a result, eggs laid on the rock have dangerously soft shells. To ensure reproductive success, ornithologists remove defective eggs from the nests to incubate them in a laboratory. When the chicks are strong enough to survive they are returned to their nests to be raised by their natural parents.

Morro Bay State Park, in the town of Morro Bay, preserves one of the largest salt marsh habitats for shore and marsh birds on this part of the coast. Camping is allowed.

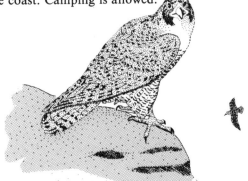

Peregrine Falcon.

Point Lobos State Reserve

TO GET THERE... it's about three miles south of Carmel and ten miles south of Monterey on Highway 1.

Cormorants, pelicans, and many other marine birds are seen on this spectacular rocky peninsula. Look for hundreds of Brandt's cormorants scooping up kelp near China Cove in spring and summer for their nests on Bird Island, a granite rock about 75 yards from shore. Also look for seals, sea lions, and sea otters.

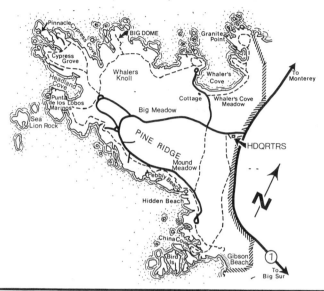

White pelicans are one of the most impressive birds to patrol our coastal waters. They are larger than brown pelicans, and unlike their brown cousins they don't plunge vertically into the water for fish. Instead, they scoop up fish while swimming.

San Luis and Merced National Wildlife Refuges

TO GET THERE... take Highway 140 west from Merced, turn left on Lander Avenue, and left of Wolfson Road to the refuge.

This is one of the Pacific Flyway's greatest concentrations of waterfowl and shorebirds, witnessing the winter passage of as many as a million ducks and 50,000 geese. Also look for dowitchers, phalaropes, black-necked stilts, burrowing owls, kestrels, and white-tailed kites. It is open from sunrise until two hours after sunset.

For more information, contact: San Luis-Merced National Wildlife Refuge, P.O. Box 2176, Los Banos, CA 93635; (209) 826-3508.

Owls have long been considered to possess supernatural powers because of their ability to see in the dark. Their eyes are so well developed that they need 100 times less light to see than we need. The largest of all owls, great horned owls feed at night on rabbits, other rodents, and birds. Because of their nocturnal manner they are heard more often than seen. Listen for a deep, resonant "Hoo, hoo-oo, hoo, hoo."

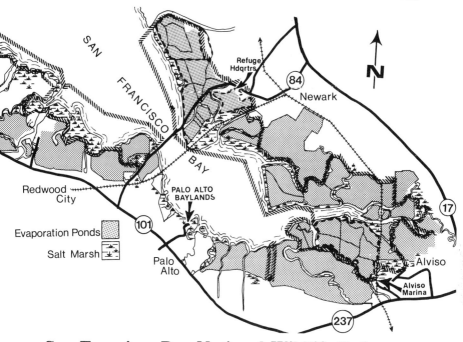

San Francisco Bay National Wildlife Refuge

TO GET THERE... refuge headquarters and visitors center are near the east end of the Dumbarton Bridge (Highway 84) in Newark.

Fortunately for the wild inhabitants of the bay, and for their human friends, the dredging, filling, diking, and polluting of the past 130 years has not destroyed the bay's entire estuarine habitat; and much of the damage done in the past can now be undone. This is the goal of the 16,000-acre San Francisco Bay National Wildlife Refuge, which comprises important wildlife habitat among the salt marshes, evaporation ponds, mudflats, and open water of the southern end of the bay.

San Francisco Bay is the largest estuary in California, and most of the shorebirds and waterfowl on the Pacific Flyway stop here at one time or another. These marshlands are the year-around home to 36 species of birds, and an important feeding and resting stopover for many more. Scientists estimate that at least 100,000 dowitchers feed here yearly, along with 1,500 avocets, and as many as 25,000 western sandpipers have been counted in these baylands in one day. More than a million shorebirds of all species are estimated to feed here in one winter season. The best time of year for seeing birds is in the fall and winter months. The refuge provides needed protection for migratory bird habitat, a small but growing harbor seal population, the rare salt marsh harvest mouse, and four rare species of birds: California clapper rails, least terns, brown pelicans, and peregrine falcons.

This is one of the nation's most unusual wildlife refuges, located in a major metropolitan area, and immediately accessible to millions of people. The refuge is people, as well as wildlife, oriented, with walking trails, viewing platforms, boardwalks, and interpretive displays. There are more than 20 miles of trails, mainly on levees.

For more information, contact: San Francisco Bay National Wildlife Refuge, P.O. Box 524, Newark, CA 94560; (415) 792-0222.

Palo Alto Baylands

TO GET THERE... from Highway 101, take Embarcadero Boulevard east to near the yacht harbor in Palo Alto.

Here you can walk an 850-foot long boardwalk through breezy fields of salt grass, pickleweed, and cordgrass to the edge of San Francisco Bay, where you will see egrets, herons, and other shore and marsh birds. You can also walk the longer, intersecting PG&E boardwalk beneath humming power lines and enjoy spacious and unusual views of the bay. This is one of the few natural wetlands to survive on this part of the bay.

The Baylands Nature Interpretive Center stands on stilts in the marsh at the beginning of the boardwalk, and has been acquainting visitors with marsh flora and fauna since it opened in 1969. A schedule of events is available from the center, including nature walks, movies, classes, and ecology workshops. For more information, call (415) 329-2506.

Farallon Islands National Wildlife Refuge

TO GET THERE... the islands begin 23 miles west of San Francisco. Boats are not allowed to land on these rocky islands, but excursions to view island wildlife are conducted by The Oceanic Society (415) 441-1106, The Point Reyes Bird Observatory (415)868-1221, The Golden Gate Chapter of the Audubon Society (415)843-2222, and other organizations.

These small, rocky islands host the largest marine birds colony south of Alaska. Hundreds of thousands of birds summer here, including auklets, oystercatchers, puffins, and murres; and the main island is the world's largest rookery for western gulls and brandt's cormorants.

These islands are one of California's most impressive wildlife

Nesting Cormorants.

Southeast Farallon Island is made of the same hard, erosion-resistant granite found in parts of Point Reyes and at Bodega Head. The buildings seen here, once a part of a U.S. government light station, are now used by scientists.

success stories. At one time the birds and mammals were slaughtered for commercial uses, or disturbed too much by human visitors to make much use of the islands. Today, these austere rocks are once again true wilderness, and with only a few people allowed to land each year — mostly scientists -- wildlife has made a phenomenal recovery. The Point Reyes Bird Observatory, which administers the islands, estimates that 75,000 common murres now visit and breed here, up from only 6,000 in the early 1960's; brandt's cormorants are found in twice the numbers seen 20 years ago; and after a hundred-year absence, rhinoceros auklets returned to breed in 1974. The islands host 12 breeding species and 350 visiting species. California sea lions and elephant seals are also common.

If you take a boat excursion to the islands, be prepared for cold winds and rough seas. September and October usually have the best weather.

Audubon Canyon Ranch
TO GET THERE... the ranch is three miles north of Stinson Beach on Highway 1 in Marin County.

Herons and egrets are among California's most majestic birds; and the best place to see them nest and mate is in the steep forested canyons east of Bolinas Lagoon. Here about 50 pair of great blue herons, and 85 pair of great egrets nest atop second-growth redwoods at the 1,300-acre Audubon Canyon Ranch.

The best time to visit the ranch is in the spring and early summer when the birds can be seen courting, building nests, and rearing their young. Because they arrive at different times through the early spring, all of these activities can sometimes be seen in one day from the ridgetop trails above Audubon Canyon. Henderson Overlook, just half a mile from the parking lot on the Alice Kent Trail, has mounted telescopes which provide excellent views into the Schwarz Grove.

The beautiful white egrets arrive in the canyon about a month after the first heron nests are built. To attract the opposite sex, egrets fan their wings, displaying their ornate mating feathers which were so prized for hats that the species was threatened with extinction around the turn of the century. Blue herons are equally impressive. They are the largest heron species in North America, standing four to five feet tall and with a wingspan of almost six feet. May is the best month to see both egrets and herons, and most of the birds are gone by late summer.

The Audubon Ranch has six miles of well-marked walking trails, including a three mile ridgetop loop trail -- combining the Alice Kent, Martin Griffin, and Bourne trails -- with lots of splendid views of Bolinas Lagoon, where the great birds feed on fish and crustaceans in the shallow water and mud. The trails pass dark, serene redwood groves and climb through stands of bay, oak, and buckeye.

Audubon Canyon Ranch has no admission charge, though donations are appreciated, and is open between March 1 and July 4 from 10 a.m. to 4 p.m. Organized groups may arrange to visit between Tuesdays and Fridays. There are picnicking facilities near the museum and bookstore. Ranch headquarters are in a two-story white house built in 1875 by Captain Peter Bourne. For more information, call (415) 383-1644.

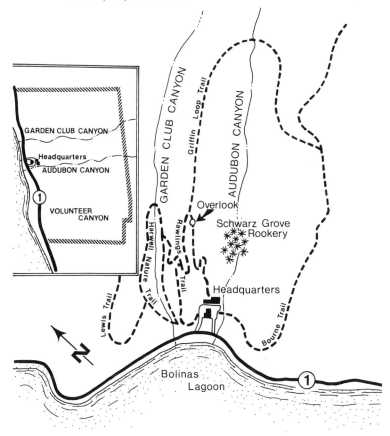

Point Reyes National Seashore

TO GET THERE... it's in Marin County, about 35 miles north of San Francisco. Take Highway 101 to the Sausalito turnoff on Highway 1, which goes west and north to the park; or take Highway 101 to San Rafael and head west on Sir Francis Drake Highway.

The Point Reyes peninsula is a beautiful and diverse land, separated from the mainland, and yielding one of the state's most fertile bird habitats. The area's forests, fields, marshlands, beaches, rocky cliffs, offshore rocks, estuaries, and ocean sustain a wonderful variety and abundance of 338 species of birds. Shore birds, marsh birds, pelagic birds, field birds, woodland birds, and raptors are all common here. Mentioned below are just a few of the places to see birds on this peninsula.

POINT REYES HEADLANDS: At the end of Sir Francis Drake Highway, 22 miles from park headquarters, the peninsula culminates at the majestic headlands near the lighthouse. These high granite cliffs plunge into the Point Reyes Headlands Research Natural Area, a virtually inaccessible rocky intertidal zone which is home to sea lions, and California murres, which nest on bare rock in summer, after spending the winter at sea. Though these black and white birds, which somewhat resemble penguins, are not graceful

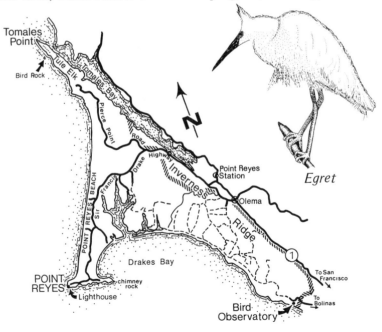

Egret

32

Common murres gather in great numbers on Bird Rock, just off-shore from Tomales Point, at Point Reyes National Seashore.

Resembling penguins, common murres stand upright and are quite sociable during the summer nesting season. They spend the rest of the year at sea.

flyers, they are powerful underwater swimmers This is the only known place in California where murres breed on the mainland. This is also one of the best places to see gray whales during their southward migration.

TOMALES POINT: This is one of the wildest and most ruggedly scenic parts of the Point Reyes peninsula. Public access is from the end of Pierce Point Road, which heads north from Sir Francis Drake Highway. Park at the old ranch buildings or at the McClures Beach parking lot and walk north. Where the point narrows to the north is an especially good place to see pelicans and cormorants. This peninsula is also home to a growing tule elk herd.

POINT REYES BIRD OBSERVATORY: There is no better way to get a close look at Point Reyes birds than to visit this observatory, which is three miles north of Bolinas via Mesa Road. Here you can see birds captured in nets, banded, and then released. Owls, hawks, finches, swallows, sparrows, warblers, and flycatchers are some of the species caught, usually between dawn and noon, as part of a variety of educational activities. The observatory is part of a non-profit organization for the conservation and observation of wild birds. It is open to the public free of charge from dawn to dusk. For more information, call: (415) 868-1221; or (415) 868-1434.

Sacramento Valley National Wildlife Refuges

TO GET THERE... these four refuges, under one administration, are in the Central Valley 50 to 90 miles north of Sacramento. The largest unit is reached by taking Old Highway 99 (Tehama Street) about six miles south from Willows.

September through January is the best time to visit these fields and wetlands. Tens of thousands of shorebirds, 300,000 geese, and more than a million ducks pass through here, making this area one of California's most important waterfowl stopovers.

These refuges have an extraordinary variety of birds, including the rare tule white-fronted geese and Aleutian Canada geese, and often have the highest count for some species during the Audubon Society Christmas bird count. Look for white-tailed kites in the willows and cottonwoods and burrowing owls. Self-guided walking and auto tours help visitors view the birds from the best places, including many good photo spots. Camping is allowed at nearby Woodson Bridge State Recreation Area.

For more information, contact: Refuge Manager, Sacramento National Wildlife Refuge, Route 1, Box 311, Willows, CA 95988; (916) 934-2801.

Great Egret.

Humboldt Bay National Wildlife Refuge
TO GET THERE... take Highway 101 from Eureka south to Hookton Road, which parallels the refuge and continues west to the county park at the beach. The refuge office is in Eureka.

A good diversity of birds visit these 8,600 acres of saltmarshes, mudflats, sandspits, and open water. Black brants, migrating by the hundreds of thousands from their Mexican wintering grounds, stop here in greatest numbers to dine mainly on the bay's abundance of eel grass. Shorebirds are common all year, and there is no shortage of ducks and whistling swans in late fall and winter. You may also see the state's second largest colony of egrets and herons in a nearby stand of Monterey cypress and eucalyptus in spring.

The preserve is open daylight hours all year and has an observation tower. For more information, contact: Humboldt Bay National Wildlife Refuge, 539 G Street, Suite 167, Eureka, CA 95501; (707) 826-3415.

Modoc National Wildlife Refuge
TO GET THERE... take Highway 395 south from Alturas, turn east on County Road 56, and south on County Road 115.

As many as 60,000 ducks, 15,000 geese, pied-billed grebes, and killdeer gather in more than 25 lakes and ponds here. These 6,283 acres of wetlands and sagebrush highlands are also the courting and nesting ground for sandhill cranes, and a stopover point for white pelicans and egrets. Probably the best time to visit is spring and fall, though bald eagles are sometimes seen in December and January. Pronghorn antelope migrate through the preserve, though it is hard to predict when they will appear. They are best seen in November and March.

For more information, contact: Modoc National Wildlife Refuge, P.O. Box 1610, Alturas, CA 96101; (916) 233-3572.
See map on page 13.

Tule Lake and Lower Klamath National Wildlife Refuges

TO GET THERE... from the town of Tulelake take East-West Road five miles west and turn south on Hill Road to refuge headquarters. From the Central Valley, the San Francisco Area, and Southern California, take Highway 5 north past Mount Shasta, turn northeast on Highway 97, and east on Highway 161.

The fall migration brings to this refuge the greatest concentration of waterfowl in North America. Early November is usually the

Flocks of Canada geese sprawl across the sky in honking chorus lines.

Principal Fall migration routes for waterfowl on the Pacific Flyway.

peak period for the migration, when more than a million ducks and geese fill the sky and the wetlands on their southward migration from as far away as Siberia and Alaska. It is not uncommon to see a quarter of a million snow geese at a time. Included in this awesome migration is 80 per cent of the world's population of Ross' geese. During a good year, 60,000 ducklings and goslings are born here.

As great as the numbers of migratory birds are now, at one time they were even greater. Less than a hundred years ago the Klamath Basin held vast lakes and marshes which attracted peak concentration of over six million waterfowl. These wet areas were filled and diked for agriculture, and today only about 20 per cent of the original wetlands remain.

Lakes, marshes, meadows, forests, farmland, and lava flows attract a wide variety of birds other than waterfowl. Sightings of more than 270 bird species have been recorded, including 180 species of nesting birds and 20 duck species. Eight species of owls and hawks nest here, as do white pelicans, great blue herons, Caspian terns, double-crested cormorants, and California and ring-billed gulls. December and January bring nearly 500 nesting bald eagles -- the largest concentration south of Alaska. Many birds of prey nest and feed at the Petroglyph Section of Lava Beds National Monument, south of the town of Tulelake. Hawks, kestrels, owls, and other raptors nest in the many holes and crevices in these cliffs, overlooking their bountiful feeding ground. Note the large quantities of rodent bones and owl pellets at the base of the cliff at the ancient Indian petroglyphs.

If you miss the fall migration, the return in spring is also worth catching, when millions of birds fly back north to the forest and tundra of Canada, Alaska, and even Siberia to build their nests and

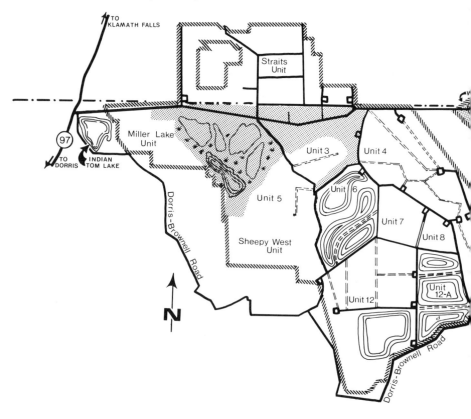

hatch their young. Snow geese migrate 3,000 miles from the Central Valley to Wrangel Island in Siberia.

There are five units of this refuge in California and Oregon, and self-guided auto tours pass Lower Klamath and Tule Lakes where there is some of the best waterfowl viewing. Some of the other roads are unimproved and may be closed during wet weather. Guided tours may be arranged for organized groups. Camping is available at Lava Beds National Monument, and there are several private trailer parks in the area. Boat rentals are also available.

For more information, contact: Refuge Manager, U.S. Fish and Wildlife Service, Route 1, Box 74, Tulelake, CA 96134; (916) 667-2231.

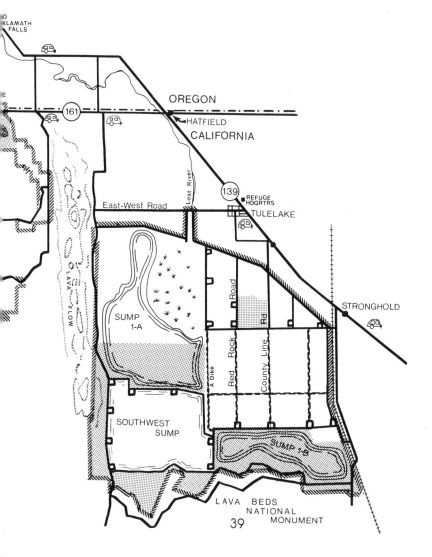

Condors

THESE GREAT BLACK BIRDS have soared the Pacific air currents since before the last ice age, their domain seemingly secure in the endless vistas of forests, mountains, and grasslands. That was before humans settled on the condor's territory, dividing it up into farms and cities, crossing it with roads and highways, and leaving little living space for creatures who cannot adapt to civilization.

With a nine-foot wingspan, the California condor is an unforgettable sight that could be gone forever by the 1990's. With numbers now below 30, this bird – the largest and rarest in North America – is on the threshold of extinction. This is not a wildlife success story; their fate now being argued by those who want to save them.

The problem is that condors aren't very compatible with civilization. They don't bother people, but people have been shooting them, poisoning them, and depriving them of habitat for more than a century. Until the 1880's, they ranged as far north as the Columbia River, and south into Mexico. Though they avoid people when possible, these large birds made easy targets, and were shot for amusement and out of misplaced fear that they may prey on livestock -- though they actually eat only carrion. Many nests were raided for eggs, and some birds were captured for zoos.

WHERE TO SEE CONDORS:

1 The Los Angeles Zoo.
2 Sespe Condor Sanctuary.
3 San Rafael Wilderness.
4 Mount Pinos and Vicinity.

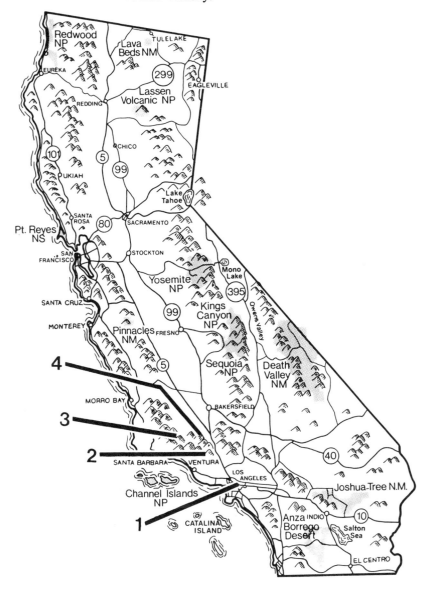

Another blow came from agricultural pesticides used in great quantities in the valleys near the condor habitat. DDT, which has since been banned, caused many condor eggs to break from calcium deficiency. Other poisons, used to control predators such as coyotes, are still being used, and have an undetermined effect on condors. Oil drilling, offroad vehicles, and subdivision have also taken their toll by violating the reclusive habitat of the condor.

For decades ornithologists advocated a hands-off policy for condor survival; but it became obvious in the 1970's that something would have to be done soon if the great birds were to be saved. Keep in mind that elephant seals, and sea otters were as close to extinction at one time, and they made stunning recoveries in this century. Unfortunately, it may not be so easy with condors since they nest only once every two years, and then only lay one egg.

The U.S. Fish and Wildlife Service is supporting a program of trapping and captive breeding that is the most ambitious government program ever to save an endangered species. They hope to increase the population to a safe level and then release birds to the wild. Biologists with the Condor Research Center in Ventura plan to attach tiny radio transmitters to some condors to monitor their movement, and to capture three condors for propagation. One will be mated with Topa Topa in the Los Angeles Zoo, and the others will be mated at the Wild Animal Park in San Diego.

CAUTION: Condors are extremely sensitive to human disturbance. To protect these endangered birds, please stay on trails and designated observation sites.

Some conservationists and biologists, however, are afraid this program might backfire by injuring wild condors, and by rearing captively born condors that will not be able to adapt to living in the wild. Instead, they advocate more habitat protection to encourage reproduction. Friends of the Earth is one of the conservation groups that vigorously opposes captive breeding, insisting that much of what a condor is comes from living in the wild. They believe that an animal raised in captivity is just a facsimile of itself. To avoid these problems, government biologists use isolation screens to keep captive condors from seeing their keepers.

Even if the captive breeding program works, these giant birds may still disappear from our state. The cause of their decline has not been alleviated, and biologists are considering releasing the offspring of captive breeding in a large protected area with appropriate rocky cliffs and a natural supply of carrion -- perhaps the Grand Canyon.

The Los Angeles Zoo
TO GET THERE... it's at Griffith Park in Los Angeles.

As of this writing, the easiest place to see a condor is at the Los Angeles Zoo in Griffith Park. Topa Topa was found injured in Topa Topa Canyon in Los Padres National Forest, and has become too tame to be returned to the wild.

Sespe Condor Sanctuary
TO GET THERE... from Ventura, take Highway 126 east to Fillmore, and head north on Goodenough and Squaw Flat roads to the trailheads. The sanctuary is an hour drive north from Los Angeles.

The rugged coastal uplands of southern Los Padres National

Condors are tragic figures in California history. How much longer they will be with us depends on what humans do in the next few years. Public support, such as that which saved the whooping cranes, is needed if this species is to survive.

Forest are prime condor habitat. This 53,000-acre sanctuary is characteristic of what the birds need for mating and raising families: steep cliffs, high summits, and solitude. The solitude is enforced by the forest service, which doesn't allow people into the sanctuary, but

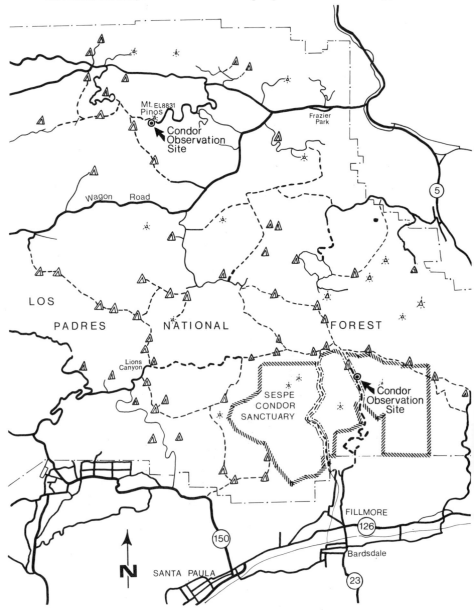

A condor chick is a very rare sight. These endangered birds raise only one young every other year, making population recovery slow and difficult.

does provide two trail corridors through it and an observation site along the Squaw Flat corridor. Here you can watch them soar overhead, sustained by Pacific breezes as they leave in search of food. There are trailcamps for backpackers just beyond the sanctuary.

Mount Pinos and Vicinity

TO GET THERE... head north from Los Angeles, or south from Bakersfield, on Highway 5, to the town of Chandler. Go west on Lockwood Ozena Road, and turn north on the narrow road up Mount Pinos.

The mountains just north and west of the Sespe sanctuary offer commanding overlooks and long views into condor country; and even if you don't see any of the great black birds, the country is so beautiful you probably won't mind very much.

The forest service has a Condor Observation Site at the summit of 8,831-foot high Mount Pinos, reached by a steep and winding dirt road. Traditionally, the second weekend in August is the time to gather atop the mountain to look for condors, though veteran birders insist that the most condor sightings are made in winter and early spring. Others tell me they are best seen between June and October. The nearby Piedra Blanca Trail makes an exceptionally scenic walk, with pine forests and views of condor habitat, and west to the Channel Islands. Trailcamps are available for backpacking.

San Rafael Wilderness

TO GET THERE... take Highway 101 north from Santa Barbara, turn east on Highway 154 (to Los Olivos), and north on Figueroa Mountain Road.

Here are 142,722 acres of some of the most rugged and remote mountains in Los Padres National Forest. This is also condor habitat, and to protect the most sensitive of the area's nesting sites, the 1,200-acre Sisquoc Condor Sanctuary was established and closed to public access.

The best way to explore this large semi-arid land is to backpack its many trails. Wilderness permits are required, and may be obtained from: San Rafael Wilderness, District Ranger, U.S. Forest Service, Star Route, Santa Barbara, CA 93105.

Elk

CENTURIES AGO, when all of California was wild, vast herds of elk migrated across the grassy valleys and wooded hills. Then during the Gold Rush a flood of settlers poured into the Golden State, cultivating and fencing the grasslands and shooting the elk for food. In a few decades the elk that once roamed in the hundreds of thousands were almost completely gone.

Today the remnant populations of tule and Roosevelt elk are increasing in numbers as they are reintroduced to some of their former habitat. Next to moose, elk are the largest members of the deer family. Human visitors should be cautious when approaching stags defending their harems during the fall rutting season, when males clash antlers in competition for cows. These antlers drop off in late winter. Females bear one or two calves in the spring.

Point Reyes National Seashore
TO GET THERE.. it's in Marin County, about 35 miles north of San Francisco. Take Highway 101 to the Sausalito turnoff on Highway 1, which goes west and north to the park; or take Highway 101 to San Rafael and head west on Sir Francis Drake Highway.

Thousands of tule elk roamed the Point Reyes peninsula for

WHERE TO SEE ELK:

1 Tule Elk Reserve State Park.
2 Owens Valley.
3 San Luis-Merced National Wildlife Refuge.

4 Point Reyes National Seashore.
5 Redwood National Park.

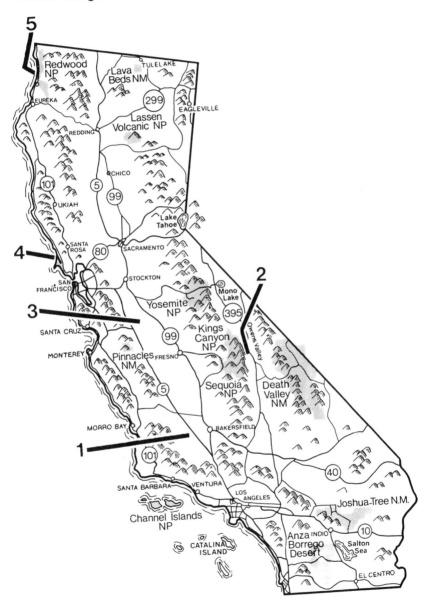

A proud tule elk surveys his magnificent realm at Point Reyes National Seashore.

eons until the last were slaughtered in the 1860's. Two bulls and eight cows were brought here in 1977 from the Owens Valley, and three more bulls were added in 1981, to roam the 2,600 acres of Tomales Point, at the north end of the national seashore. As of 1983 their number had increased to 30 and they show every indication of thriving. Eight calves were born in the spring of 1982. To see them, take Sir Francis Drake Highway north from park headquarters, and take Pierce Point Road north. Bring binoculars and water, and be ready for cool, windy weather.

Deer, the smaller cousins of elk, are also common on the Point Reyes Peninsula. In addition to the native mule deer, you may also see the white to beige fallow deer, native to southern Europe, and the spotted axis deer from India. Dr. Millard Ottinger, a local rancher, introduced these beautiful exotic deer to the area west of the Inverness Ridge in the 1940's and '50's. These deer are easy to see because they don't blend into their adopted habitat, and also because there are so many of them. They are doing so well here that eventually the national park service will have to deal with the tough question of controlling their numbers. The best place to see them is in the wilderness area south of Limantour Road.

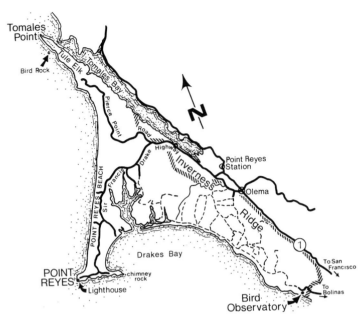

The largest elk in California, Roosevelt elk live in the foggy, rainy, north coast region.

Redwood National Park
TO GET THERE... the Prairie Creek unit of this park is six miles north of Orick on Highway 1.

Larger than the tule elk, the Roosevelt elk strikes an impressive pose in its green and foggy realm in California's north coast redwood country. Also known as wapati, these elk once roamed in vast herds. Today, a few small remnant herds remain in the Prairie Creek Redwoods State Park unit of Redwood National Park, and among the coastal forests of Six Rivers National Forest. Two distinct herds are found at Prairie Creek Redwoods: One at the meadow along Prairie Creek just south of Elk Prairie Campground near Highway 101; and the other in the meadows at the foot of Gold Bluff Beach.

Prairie Creek Redwoods is one of three state parks included in Redwood National Park, which stretches 46 miles along the coast and has some of the most impressive stands of the world's tallest trees.

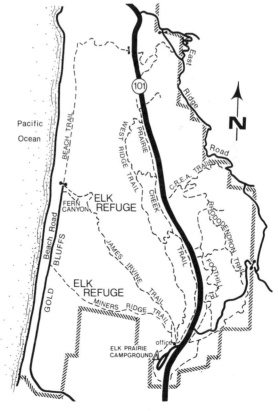

Owens Valley

TO GET THERE.. this long valley lies just east of the Sierra Nevada, and is transected by Highway 395.

Fifty-five tule elk were introduced here from the Central Valley in 1933. They roam freely over a large area, to an altitude of up to 8,000 feet in the Inyo National Forest, and between Lone Pine and Bishop. The largest free-roaming group of these elk in the state, they are often seen along the Owens River and in the Poverty Hills and Red Mountain area. The state fish and game commission is using controlled hunts to limit the elk population to between 250 and 300 animals.

Tule Elk Reserve State Park

TO GET THERE... it is 25 miles west of Bakersfield, near Tupman. From Highway 5 take the Stockdale Highway exit and continue on Morris Road 1.5 miles to Station Road, and turn right to the viewing area.

This preserve covers 965 acres of the tule elks' native Central Valley habitat. Elk are easily seen at the 2 p.m. feeding time. For more information, write to Tule Elk Reserve State Park, P.O. Box 126, Tupman, CA 93276; (805) 765-5004.

Tule elk in the Central Valley live a rather domestic existence.

52

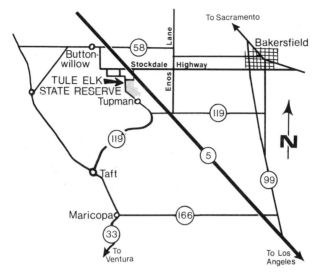

San Luis--Merced National Wildlife Refuge

**TO GET THERE... take Highway 140 west from Merced, turn left
on Lander Avenue, and left on Wolfson Road to the refuge.**

A small herd of tule elk can be seen here in their natural habitat.
For more information write to San Luis--Merced National Wildlife
Refuge, P.O. Box 2176, Los Banos, CA 93635; (209) 826-3508.

Monarch Butterflies

ONE OF NATURE'S great mysteries, monarch butterflies breeze over the mountains and valleys of California, from as far away as Canada, to settle on their favorite groves of pine, cypress, and eucalyptus on the California coast. Of the many millions that begin the journey each fall, relatively few reach their destination. Their fragile bodies are often destroyed by weather, eaten by predators, or thrown hopelessly off course; and it's amazing that any of them make it to their destinations. How they navigate is still a mystery.

These orange and black butterfies lay their eggs on milkweed, a perennial herb, and monarch larvae consume immense quantities of the plant's leaves. Fortunately, milkweed has no economic value, so they aren't regarded as a pest. When butterflies emerge from the pupae, they migrate to milder climates where they gather on narrow-leaf trees for the winter.

Monarch butterflies are beautiful, but capricious. You may see impressive concentrations of them or only a few, and there is no guarantee of seeing a good display even at their favorite places. On sunny and mildly warm days the insects open their resplendent wings and flutter around the groves. This is the time to see them. Butterfly-watching isn't nearly as rewarding on cool and overcast days when they cling to the trees with wings folded. With this in mind, here are

WHERE TO SEE MONARCH BUTTERFLIES:

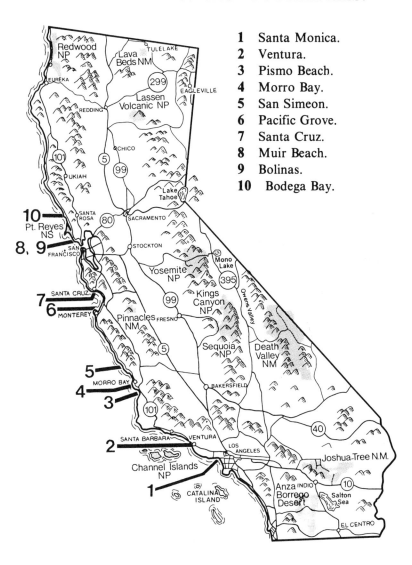

1 Santa Monica.
2 Ventura.
3 Pismo Beach.
4 Morro Bay.
5 San Simeon.
6 Pacific Grove.
7 Santa Cruz.
8 Muir Beach.
9 Bolinas.
10 Bodega Bay.

Monarch butterflies on a cypress tree.

some of the best places to see them from south to north:

SANTA MONICA: Monarchs gather in a small grove of pine and eucalyptus about 12 miles north of Santa Monica and two miles inland.

VENTURA: Nature walks are conducted to congregations of butterflies in several groves. For information, contact: Ventura Chamber of Commerce, P.O. Box 1058, Ventura, CA 93002.

PISMO BEACH: Look for monarchs in the eucalyptus trees at the North Beach Campground, on the west side of Highway 1. It's near the Grover City-Pismo Beach city limits.

MORRO BAY: Monarchs may be seen in the eucalyptus trees between campsites 100 and 114 in Morro Bay State Park. Ask at the natural history museum for information on butterfly walks.

SAN SIMEON: Butterflies concentrate in the eucalyptus and cypress trees around the old Sebastian Store (built in 1852).

PACIFIC GROVE: The Butterfly Parade, on the second Saturday of October commemorates the arrival of the monarchs. You can see them at Milar's Butterfly Grove Motel (park at Ridge Road, south of Lighthouse Avenue); Butterfly Trees Lodge; a six-acre grove at the west end of Lighthouse Avenue; and at George Washington Park. The butterflies are a major tourist attraction, and are strictly protected by city ordinance. For more information see the natural history museum at the intersection of Forest and Central avenues.

SANTA CRUZ: Off Highway 1, near the northern end of Santa Cruz, Natural Bridges State Beach has a eucalyptus grove that is popular with monarch butterflies. Rangers will direct you to the Monarch Trail, an easy walk through the area's most popular butterfly hangouts, beginning in early October.

MUIR BEACH: From Highway 1 in Marin County, take Pacific Way west and just beyond Redwood Creek to the Elizabeth Terwilliger Butterfly Grove in a stand of Monterey pines.

BOLINAS: Near the intersection of Terrace and Ocean avenues, monarchs cluster in a eucalyptus grove at the two-acre Audubon Monarch Butterfly Grove.

BODEGA BAY: Butterflies gather in a cypress grove just north of town on Highway 1.

Mountain Sheep

T HE MOUNTAIN SHEEP of California live only in the wildest and most inaccessible places, requiring true wilderness, and will not tolerate human disturbance. These hooved mountaineers nego-tiate precarious granite precipices as if to defy gravity and are a truly startling sight for mountain travelers.

Once numbering in the tens of thousands, the Sierra bighorn now are fewer than 400 individuals in five herds between Convict Creek and Mount Whitney in the southern Sierra, and in the Warner Mountains. The desert variety is more numerous, but still only a remnant of what they were a century ago.

Bighorns are so sensitive to man's presence, and so vulnerable to disease carried by domestic livestock, poaching, and loss of habitat, that their fate is still uncertain. For 150 years they have been retreating to the most remote mountain areas; and it has only been in the last decade that their condition has begun to improve. Attempts to reintroduce them to their former habitat have met with mixed results. A band of bighorn transplanted to Lava Beds National Monument, for example, was ravaged by disease; but an effort to repopulate the Warner Mountains--in northeastern California-- and

WHERE TO SEE BIGHORN SHEEP:

1 Anza Borrega Desert State Park.
2 Joshua Tree National Monument.
3 San Gorgonio Wilderness.
4 Cucamonga Wilderness.

5 Death Valley National Monument.
6 Mount Langly.
7 California Bighorn Zoological Area.
8 South Warner Wilderness.

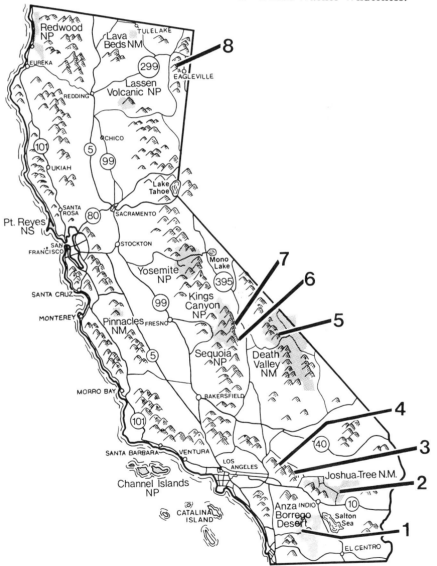

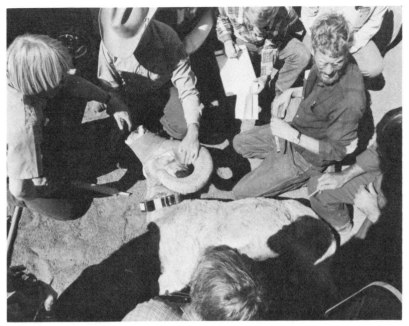

Scientists attaching a radio collar to a Sierra bighorn. This kind of research tells us where this threatened species lives and what habitat needs protection.

near Mount Langley--in the southern Sierra--now appears to be successful.

Bighorns are among the state's most difficult large mammals to see in the wild. First you must go where they live, which usually requires vigorous backpacking or day hiking into some of California's steepest and most difficult terrain. Then you must keep a very close watch, preferably with binoculars, for movement on the mountain slopes. Bighorns range from light to dark brown, with white rumps, and are amazingly well camouflaged in their natural habitat. You could easily look in their direction and not see them. Their acutely-sharp vision usually lets them see you long before you see them.

Rams weigh twice as much as ewes and are identified by heavy, spiral horns used for ritualized mating and territorial bouts. The intense, sharp sound of two rams battering their heads together often resonates through the mountain canyons, and it is only because of their specially reinforced skulls that their heads don't shatter on impact. In fact, they rarely show any sign of ill effects. Ewes normally bear only one lamb at a time, though sometimes two are born--usually in May and June-- and grow fast enough to follow their mothers in two or three days. Mountain sheep may live as many as 17 years, and their age is determined by growth rings in their horns.

Bighorns are always alert. They eat grasses, herbs, and leaves quickly, and chew later when they are in safe places. Their main predators are coyotes, mountain lions, and humans, and are most vulnerable when they come down from their high mountain sanctuaries to feed at lower elevations where there is less snow. When threatened, they can gallop at 35 miles per hour even on steep terrain, aided by hooves that are curved inward on the bottoms for gripping rock. Desert bighorns are usually seen not far from mountain springs.

Access to bighorn country is sometimes restricted because of their sensitivity to human presence. When traveling in their domain respect their special needs by enjoying them from a distance.

California Bighorn Sheep Zoological Area
TO GET THERE... it is located in the John Muir Wilderness, just east of Sequoia and Kings Canyon national parks. Road access to trailheads is from Highway 395 near Independence, in the Owens Valley.

The largest herds of Sierra bighorns are found in the 41,000 acres of the California Bighorn Sheep Zoological Area on the Sierra crest surrounding Mount Baxter and Mount Williamson. In summer they dwell among the high passes and peaks of some of the country's highest mountains—some of which exceed 14,000 feet. In winter they descend to places of shallow snow where they can forage for food; and may be seen in the foothills near Independence.

The Zoological Area, in the John Muir Wilderness, was established in 1971 jointly by the California Department of Fish and Game, the National Park Service, and the U.S. Department of Forestry. Before its creation bighorns had to compete with domestic livestock for grazing room. Now, domestic animals are prohibited, hunting is more strictly controlled, and no more than 25 people per day may use foot trails through the preserves. Bighorns may be seen on Mount Langley, Baxter Pass, Mount Gould, and on the Bighorn Plateau in summer, and often cross over the crest of the range into the national parks.

Visitor access is limited to the Shepherd, Baxter, and Sawmill

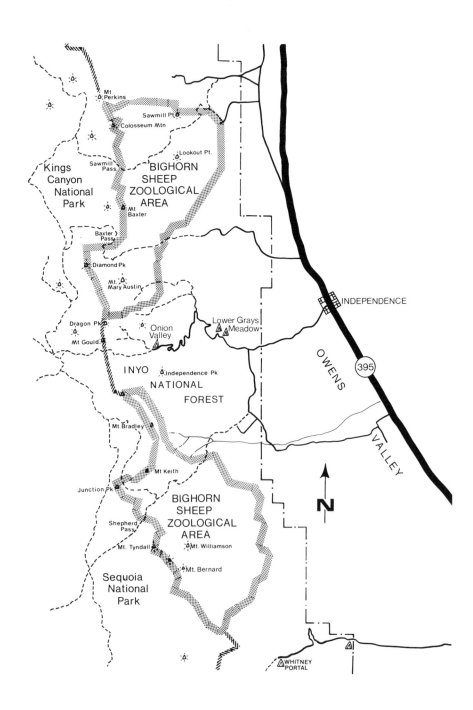

Mt Perkins

Sawmill Pt.

Colosseum Mtn

Lookout Pt.

Kings Canyon National Park

Sawmill Pass

BIGHORN SHEEP ZOOLOGICAL AREA

Mt Baxter

Baxter Pass

Diamond Pk

Mt. Mary Austin

Dragon Pk

Onion Valley

Lower Grays Meadow

INDEPENDENCE

Mt Gould

INYO

NATIONAL

FOREST

Independence Pk

OWENS

Mt Bradley

Mt Keith

395

Junction Pk

BIGHORN SHEEP ZOOLOGICAL AREA

N

Shepherd Pass

VALLEY

Mt. Tyndall

Mt. Williamson

Mt. Bernard

Sequoia National Park

WHITNEY PORTAL

Pass trails. For permits and information, contact the Visitors Information Center in Lone Pine, (619) 876-4252; or the U.S. Forest Service ranger station, (619) 876-5542.

Anza Borrega Desert State Park
TO GET THERE... go 94 miles northeast of San Diego via Highway 78.

This half million acres of desert wilderness is by far the largest state park in California. Less than a three-hour drive from Southern California cities, this is an excellent destination for camping, walk-

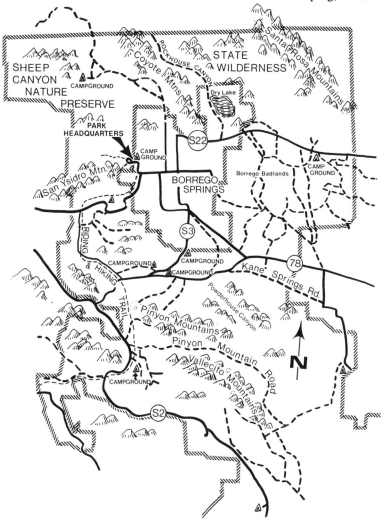

ing, and nature study, especially from about November to May. There are still desert bighorns in the remote mountains of the northern part of the park, and especially in the Santa Rosa Mountains, which rise to more than 8,000 feet. Hardy hikers may explore their domain in the Sheep Canyon Natural Preserve, and the Santa Rosa Mountains State Wilderness. Hiking and backpacking in these areas is difficult, though, because of the lack of water and trails. During dry spells bighorns are sometimes seen at the spring in Borrego Palm Canyon, near park headquarters and Palm Canyon Campground. Sheep are most easily seen during dry periods, especially in summer, when they come down to springs to drink. They can go three days without water. Also look for them in the San Ysidro Mountains, near park headquarters.

For additional information, contact: Anza Borrego Desert State Park, P.O. Box 428, Borrego Springs, CA 92004; (619) 767-5311.

A desert bighorn.

San Gorgonio Wilderness

TO GET THERE... in San Bernardino County, it may be reached by way of Highway 38.

This 34,644-acre mountain wilderness ranges from desert to the alpine ecology of 11,502-foot San Gorgonio Mountain. A small number of bighorns inhabit this area, though they are hard to find. They are strictly protected by law. For permits and information, contact: San Gorgonio Wilderness, District Ranger, Mill Creek Ranger Station, San Bernardino National Forest, Route 1, Box 264, Mentone, CA 92359; (714) 794-1123.

Cucamonga Wilderness Area

TO GET THERE... it's north of San Bernardino by way of Riverside Drive, which turns into Lytle Creek Road. Stop at the ranger station for further instructions and wilderness permits.

This is the best place near the Los Angeles area to observe bighorns. Though this steep and rugged piece of the San Gabriel Mountains covers less than 10,000 acres, it is remote and wild enough to support several bands of sheep. For wilderness permits and information, contact: Cucamonga Wilderness Supervisor, San Bernardino National Forest, 144 North Mountain View Avenue, San Bernardino, CA 92408; (714) 383-5588, or (714) 887-2576.

Joshua Tree National Monument

TO GET THERE.. the monument is 140 miles east of Los Angeles. take Highway 10 east, and turn north on Twentynine Palms Highway (Highway 62) to the park's north entrance roads at the towns of Joshua Tree and Twentynine Palms. The south entrance is at Cottonwood Springs via Highway 10.

This is a large, high desert park, with nearly half a million acres of designated wilderness that is home to a wide variety of desert animals--coyotes being exceptionally abundant. This rugged and ecologically diverse land ranges from an elevation of 1,000 feet in the Colorado Desert to the east to nearly 6,000 feet in the Mohave Desert to the west. You may be able to find several herds of mountain sheep between Twentynine Palm and Pinto Wye Junction and around Hidden Valley and Wonderland of Rocks. Remember, they blend into the desert and are hard to see. For camping and other information, contact: Joshua Tree National Monument, 74485 National Monument Drive, Twentynine Palms, CA 92266; (619) 794-1123.

Death Valley National Monument

TO GET THERE... it is reached from the north and east over Highway 95, and from the south and west over Highways 127, 178, and 190.

This is the largest national park unit in California. It is also one of the most ecologically diverse, ranging from high mountain pine forests to barren salt flats. Though one of their last strongholds, there are now estimated to be fewer than 600 desert bighorn sheep left in the park.

Some wildlife biologists blame burros for the decline, insisting that they forage on many of the same plants and foul many of the waterholes used by bighorns. Charles B. Hunt, author of *Death Valley* (U.C. Press, 1975) disagrees with the prevailing view, main-

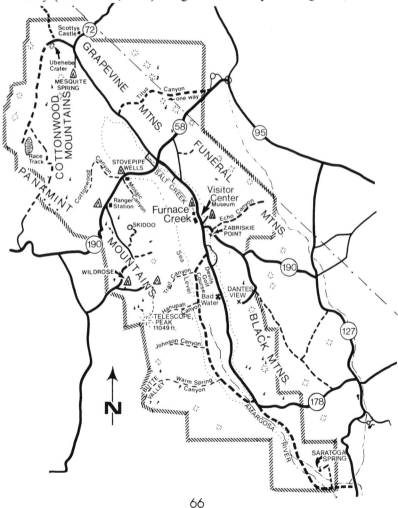

taining that burros and bighorns inhabit different areas. He claims that burros, introduced by miners in the nineteenth century, live mostly on areas of the smoother Pre-Cambrian and Cambrian rock, while bighorns prefer places of Paleozoic rock which are too jagged for burros' hooves. He points to archaeological evidence indicating that bighorns were never common on the Pre-Cambrian and Cambrian formations. He does admit, however, that burros denude their range when their population is too high. The national park service has an adoption program for keeping their numbers down, and hopes to eliminate them completely in the 1980's.

Willow Springs, in the Black Mountains is a good place to look for sheep. The road to this area is rough, but passable by a car with high clearance (check current conditions). Walk the streambed at least half a mile from road's end. Wahguyhe Peak is another area frequented by desert sheep. The dirt road to this area is also rough.

Because desert sheep rarely wander far from water, many of the springs in the steep mountains of the Death Valley area offer good sighting possibilities. Being one of the hottest places in the world in summer, the best time to visit is between November and May. There are a wide variety of accommodations, from primitive camping to luxury hotels; and there are enough interesting things to see and do to last at least a week. For more information, contact: Superintendent, Death Valley National Monument, Death Valley, CA 92328; (619) 786-2331.

South Warner Wilderness

TO GET THERE... in the northeast corner of the state, trail access is from near Jess Valley, off Highway 395, and from near Eagleville, on Highway 81.

This rugged, forested wilderness is the home of a growing band of transplanted mountain sheep. In 1980 ten bighorns were brought from the southern Sierra, four from Canada, and five survivors from an unsuccessful repopulation program at Lava Beds National Monument, to the west. These 70,000 acres of protected wilderness are ideal bighorn country, and the band seems to be doing well and reproducing normally.

In summer they dwell higher on the east side of the crest of the range, dominated by 9,906-foot Eagle Peak. This is a lush, forested land of mountains, meadows, lakes, and waterfalls--ideal for backpacking. Ewes and lambs are usually found at lower elevations, with rams ranging nearer the crest. A good trail system parallels both

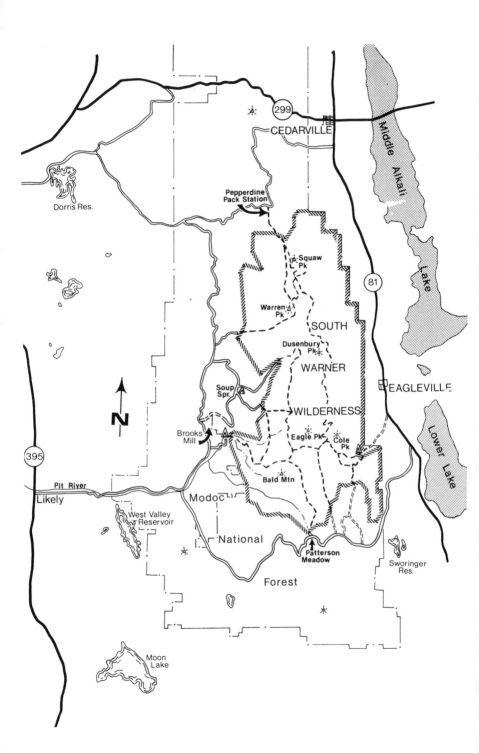

Desert bighorn.

sides of the mountain crest. The Summit Trail journeys 27 miles from Patterson Meadow in the south to Pepperdine Camp in the north. The Owl Creek Trail runs the east face of the range. During winter, when heavy snows blanket the range, bighorns come down the slopes to graze within view of Highway 81 near Eagleview. They are also sometimes seen from the highway in summer, though farther up the slopes.

A good way to locate sheep is with a spotting scope or binoculars from Highway 81, and then to climb the steep mountainside, where you may be able to approach within a quarter of a mile of the band. These are the most accessible wild bighorns in the state. For wilderness permits and other information, contact: South Warner Wilderness, Modoc National Forest, P.O. Box 220, Cedarville, CA 96104: 916 279—6116.

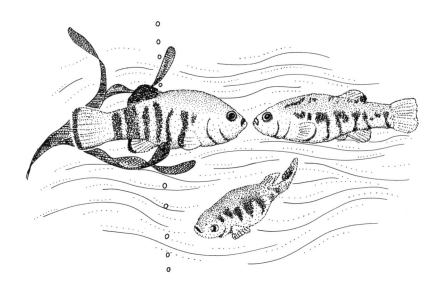

Pupfish

THERE ARE FISH that are bigger and more beautiful, but none that are more remarkable than the little desert pupfish of Death Valley. First, let's consider where they live. Death Valley lies in the southeast part of the state, shielded from moist Pacific air by some of the nation's highest mountains, and is one of the driest and hottest places in the world. With annual rainfall averaging less than two inches this would seem to be the last place to look for fish. The meager and salty bodies of water found in this arid land probably form the most restricted habitat of any wild animal in the world.

To understand how a fish can survive in saline water that is often only a few inches deep, and in some places has the water capacity of a bathtub, we need to look at the history of this amazing fish.

Twenty thousand years ago Death Valley was very different. The climate was moist and cool; the hills were green; and the High Sierra was capped with glacial ice. Camels, mastadons, and saber-toothed tigers were among an abundance of wildlife in this verdant land. At that time there was a large freshwater lake in the valley that is now called Lake Manly. Then there was only one species of pupfish, and it was a freshwater species which also lived in the Colorado River and many other streams and lakes. But when the ice age ended, and the climate turned dry, pupfish became isolated in

Lake Manly when a drainage connecting it with the Colorado River dried up. When the lake disappeared about nine to ten thousand years ago, and when a smaller lake dried up only two thousand years ago, the little remaining water turned salty and the few surviving pupfish were isolated into four populations in what is now Death Valley. There are five additional populations outside the national monument.

The one-and-a-half inch pupfish was one of the few freshwater creatures in the valley, and the only fish, to adapt to saltwater. What happened was an extremely rapid rate of evolution. Dr. James Deacon of the University of Nevada termed these fish "the Darwin

WHERE TO SEE PUPFISH:

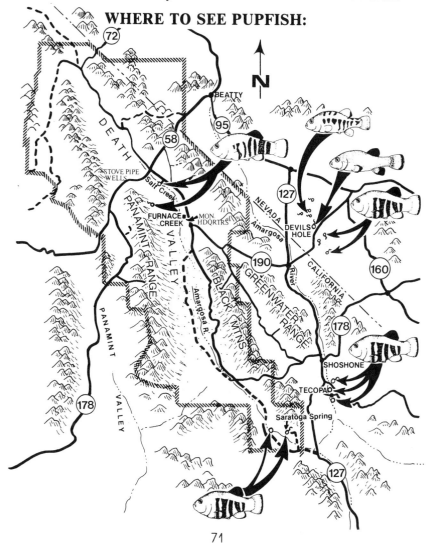

finches of the desert" by demonstrating what Charles Darwin noticed in the Galapagos Islands -- that animals evolve to adapt to changing environments. These pupfish, however, also demonstrate a lesson that even Darwin missed, that evolution doesn't have to be a long, slow process over millions of years. Dr. Steven M. Stanley of John Hopkins University, author of *The New Evolutionary Timetable,* said that these little fish may be the best living example of rapid evolution, which is now called the theory of "punctuated equilibrium." This theory states that evolution is characterized by long periods of relative stability broken by short bursts of change. In a few thousand years one species evolved into five in the Death Valley area because genetic change can happen quickly among small populations where a few mutations can have a dramatic effect on the whole gene pool. By reaching maturity in only two to three months, cyprinodon can further accelerate their rate of evolution by producing several generations per year.

These little fish are also of scientific interest because of the unusually wide range of temperatures and salinity in which they have adapted. As adaptable as these creatures are, they are now threatened by human activities. Since the 1940's, eight populations have disappeared because of the construction of bathhouses at the source of thermal springs, the introduction of predatory fish, the draining of springs for agriculture, and by groundwater pumping that lowers the water table.

Death Valley National Monument
TO GET THERE... it is reached from the north and east over Highway 95, and from the south and west over Highways 127, 178, and 190. It's in the southeast part of the state.
SALT CREEK: Take the half mile boardwalk nature trail through the pickleweed and cordgrass saltmarsh along this salty little creek that flows about two miles. Look for fish in the deeper pools, but if you don't see any, they may be farther upstream. When the water is cold in winter the fish are dormant in the bottom mud, and hard to see. They become more active in spring when the water warms and they can be seen feeding on brown and green algae. As the pools dry out in summer most fish die, leaving only the hardiest few to carry on in the remaining pools.
AMARGOSA RIVER: This small stream flows through the watercourse remnant of an ice age river. Nearby Shoreline Butte still shows terraces formed by successive levels of prehistoric Lake

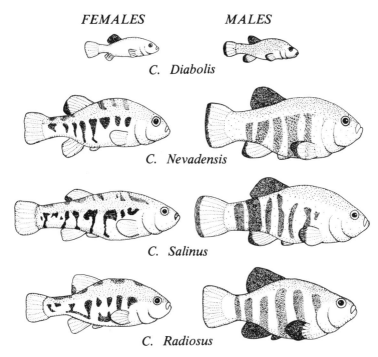

FEMALES   *MALES*

C. *Diabolis*

C. *Nevadensis*

C. *Salinus*

C. *Radiosus*

Manly. Pools in the stream are home of the pupfish species cyprinodon nevadensis amargosae.

SARATOGA SPRING: Here are three ponds used by wintering waterfowl and the pupfish species cyprinodon nevadensis.

COTTONBALL MARSH: At the east foot of Tucki Mountain, is the largest marsh on the salt pan, with pools encrusted with salt and gypsum. Look for pupfish in the 12-to-18-inch deep pools among the pickleweed and salt grass. The marsh lies below sea level.

If you don't see pupfish in these places, check the aquarium at the visitors Center Museum at Furnace Creek.

Sea Otters

SEA OTTERS ARE endlessly fascinating to watch. They frolic in the waves, dive for food, care for their young, and crack shellfish open with stones while floating on their backs. Otters spend an amazing amount of time eating, and after a few hours of watching them you might conclude that their 175-mile stretch of coast is their sea food smorgasbord. They also enjoy grooming themselves and each other, and caressing their young, who grow up with lots of affection. Young otters, and older ones too, love to play, and especially seem to enjoy games involving kelp. You might even conclude that they live a nearly ideal existence.

Once sea otters numbered in the hundreds of thousands from Baja California to the Aleutian Islands. They were a common sight off our coast until their thick, soft fur was discovered by Spanish, Russian, and American fur traders. It has been estimated that more than one million pelts were taken between 1740 and 1911, when they were nearly extinct. These otters were thought to be completely gone from the California coast until a small group was found at the mouth of Bixby Creek, along the Big Sur coast, in 1938 during construction of Highway 1.

WHERE TO SEE SEA OTTERS:

1 Montana De Oro State Park.

2 William Randolph Hearst Beach.

3 Little John State Park.

4 Julia Pfeiffer Burns State Park.

5 Pfeiffer Big Sur State Park.

6 Garrapata State Park.

7 Point Lobos State Reserve.

8 Monterey Peninsula.

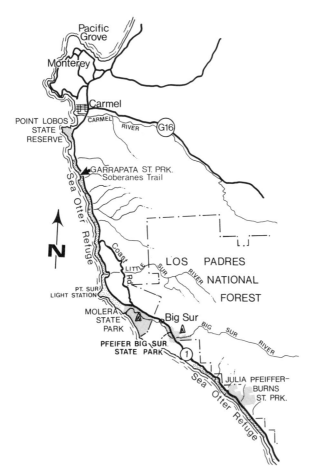

Listed as "threatened" under the Endangered Species Act, there are now only about 1,500 of the furry shellfish eaters, and their numbers have increased little if any since 1973. Friends of the Sea Otter, a Monterey-based conservation group, claims that the otter population has stopped growing and that these amiable creatures should be classified "endangered", to add protection from those who think there are too many of them. They insist that as a natural part of the nearshore kelp community, otters should not be restricted in their distribution along the coast, and in fact, should be reintroduced to additional parts of their natural range. Commercial shellfish interests are working to have them delisted in order to allow limits on the range and numbers of otters. In other words, they want to do away with the competition.

Sea otters more closely resemble land dwellers than any other marine mammal. Members of the mustelid family, they are close relatives of river otters, weasels, skunks, and badgers. Their dexterous, five-fingered forepaws are perfect for holding seashells, but are webbed enough for easy underwater swimming, and seem to be evolving into flippers. Unlike their terrestrial cousins, sea otters are awkward on land, and come ashore only to give birth, escape from enemies, and to find refuge from severe storms. The smallest of the marine mammals, they weigh 60 to 80 pounds when mature and measure from about four to five feet in length.

Sea otters live in kelp beds, which are the tops of large submerged kelp forests. Growing rapidly in areas of shallow water, this large marine algae is useful to otters in many ways: it helps to hide them from sharks; it forms the habitat for much of their food; they wrap themselves and their young in it to keep from drifting away in their sleep; and it makes the coast more habitable by mitigating the force of waves. Otters, in turn, benefit kelp by eating algae eaters such as abalone, snails, and especially sea urchins. Don't let their teddy-bear looks deceive you; these little fellows can really eat --

A hungry otter with a large sea urchin for lunch.

about 25 percent of their body weight every day. Otters not only shuck clam and oyster shells with rocks placed on their stomachs while floating on their backs, they also use rock tools as hammers and chisels to remove abalone and other bottom-feeding shellfish from underwater rocks. They can dive as deep as 300 feet for food.

Mating may occur any time of year and is always done in water. After an eight to 12 month gestation period, females usually bear only one pup every other year. The main pupping period is from December through March, peaking in February. You will probably see mothers and babies together. They are famous for their parental

SEA OTTERS IN PERIL!

Despite state and federal protection, the sea otter population has increased little if any since 1973, and may actually be declining. The 1982 sea otter census produced a count of only 1,194 otters (excluding dependent pups). Biologists still have no definitive explanation, yet some disturbing trends are now apparent. The number of dead sea otters recovered along the coast has increased significantly during the last few years. In addition to those killed by natural causes -- mainly by disease and predation by sharks -- there has been a sharp increase in carcasses found to have been shot and drowned in fishing nets, particularly in the southern part of their range, where conflicts with shellfisheries are most intense. Pesticides, heavy metals, and other pollutants may also be taking a toll.

Efforts to open sea otter habitat to offshore oil drilling pose the greatest potential threat to otter survival. More than any other marine mammals, sea otters are vulnerable to oil spills because they are the only ones to rely on fur for insulation. When as little as 30 percent of their fur is matted with oil, they lose more heat than their bodies can produce, resulting in death by hypothermia. And to make matters worse there are commercial interests trying to remove what little protection these native mammals now enjoy. A group of commercial shellfishermen called Save Our Shellfish, with support from the oil and gas industry, and legal advice from the powerful Pacific Legal Foundation, is lobbying to restrict sea otter habitat.

With all these threats, otters need all the friends they can get. Friends Of The Sea Otter, a 4,500-member conservation group, works to protect sea otters and their coastal habitat with direct political action and public education. For more information, contact: Friends Of The Sea Otter, P.O. Box 221220, Carmel, CA 93022; (408) 625-3290.

affection, and mothers teach their young nearly everything they need to know to survive in the community of otters: what to eat, how to gather it, how to avoid danger, and even how to swim. Males roam more than females, and predominate at the species' northern and southern range limits.

The best way to see sea otters is to visit their 175 miles of coastal habitat between Monterey and San Luis Obispo and to scan the kelp beds with binoculars or a telescope. Brownish patches floating on the water are kelp beds, and otters are seen as bobbing brown chunks. Because otters are sometimes hard to distinguish from kelp bulbs, binoculars are nearly indispensable. Even before you see them, their presence may be known by the sharp sound of sea shells cracking against rock, or by high-pitched cooing and squealing sounds. Hungry gulls also sometimes mark the whereabouts of feeding otters as they wait to clean up the leftovers. In the fall the ocean is calm enough for the kelp, and otters, to gather near shore. During stormy weather and rough seas, otters congregate in protected coves and bays. Look for otters in groups, called "rafts", which usually contain two to six otters, and rarely more than 16.

Naturalist-led field trips to study and observe sea otters and other marine life are offered by the University of California Extension Services in Berkeley and Santa Cruz. For more information, call U.C. Santa Cruz at (408) 429-2761; or U.C. Berkeley at (415) 642-4111.

Here are some of the best places to watch sea otters:

Montana De Oro State Park
TO GET THERE... it's at the end of Pecho Road, about seven miles south of Los Osos.

This spectacular and wild stretch of coast has lots of rocky overlooks for watching sea otter, sea lions, seals, and other marine life. Camping facilities are provided.

San Luis Obispo County
North from Cambria, Highway 1 is reunited with the ocean, providing many roadside turnoffs where otters are seen. Also look for them at the pier at William Randolph Hearst Memorial State Beach, near the town of San Simeon.

Mother and pup.

The Big Sur Coast

Between San Simeon and Carmel Highway 1 grasps the mountainous coast, unfolding new and impressive panoramas with every turn in the road. There are many turnoffs to stop and look at scenery, and to watch sea otters. The best places to look are where the road dips down toward the sea at the mouths of valleys -- especially at bridges. Scan the kelp beds at the mouth of Bixby Creek, where the few surviving otters were discovered in 1938. They may also be seen at Little John State Reserve, Julia Pfeiffer-Burns State Park (with campground), Pfeiffer Big Sur State Park (with campground), and Andrew Molera State Park (with campground). Pfeiffer Big Sur is mostly an inland park, but there is a wonderful beach frequented by otters at the end of Sycamore Canyon Road, which intersects Highway 1.

Garrapata State Park

TO GET THERE... the Soberanes Trail begins 4.6 miles south of the entrance to Point Lobos, on Highway 1. Look for a cypress grove at the trailhead.

A 1.2-mile long cliff-top trail offers spectacular Big Sur seascape views on its way south to the rocky promontory called Soberanes Point. This is an easy trail, and sea otters and sea lions can be easily seen. A small sandy beach is perfect for picnicking, and nearby tidepools are worth exploring. Eventually the trail will stretch for four miles to the beach at Garrapata Creek. For updated information, call park headquarters at (408) 667-2315.

Point Lobos State Reserve

TO GET THERE... drive three miles south of Carmel and ten miles south of Monterey on Highway 1.

This 1,500-acre rocky peninsula is world-renowned for its scenery. The park's six miles of granite promontories and sheltered inlets are home to about 70 sea otters, which may be found in all parts of the preserve. They may be seen from the higher overlooks, especially in the kelp beds of the coves north of Sea Lion Point. In the southern part of the preserve, toward Bird Rock, the cliffs aren't as high, and you can see then at a closer range. Climb to rock overlooks between Sand Hill Cove and China Cove. During rough weather otters congregate in protected coves. Mother and baby otters are often seen in late spring at Headland Cove and Whaler's Cove. Also look for

sea lions, harbor seals, and sea birds. For more information, call:
(408) 649-4909.

The rugged, rocky seascape of Point Lobos is one of the state's most fertile marine wildlife habitats.

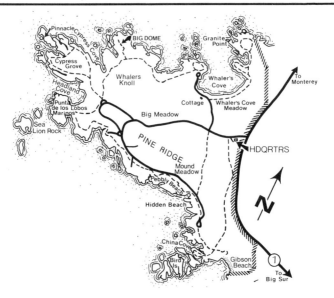

Monterey Peninsula

This is the most populous part of the sea otter domain; but even here they can be seen close up. You might want to start out with a visit to the Friends of the Sea Otter Center, at the Barnyard Shopping Center, just east of Highway 1 on Carmel Valley Road in Carmel. The center has booklets and information and is open daily from 11 a.m. to 3 p.m. Their phone number is (408) 625-3290. Another way to view sea otters, and sea lions, is to take weekend boat tours from Monterey's Fisherman's Wharf. You may even see them from the wharf itself.

Here are some places to look on the peninsula:

1) Monterey Wharf
2) Fisherman's Wharf
3) Coast Guard Breakwater
4) Lovers Point
5) Otter Point
6) Point Pinos
7) Point Joe
8) Cypress Point
9) Pescadero Point

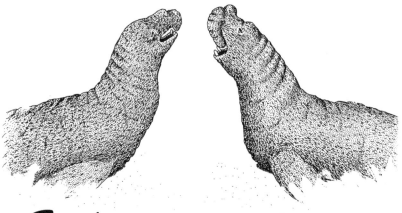

Seals and sea lions

SEALS AND SEA LIONS ARE near the top of the list of wildlife favorites; and California is one of the best places in the world to see them. From San Diego to Del Norte counties you can watch them sleep on offshore rocks, play in the surf, and bark out their greetings. These flipper-footed mammals (pinnipeds) are now such an intrinsic part of coastal California that it is hard to imagine that at one time many of them seemed doomed to extinction.

In the early years of this century elephant seals were down to less than a dozen individuals; northern fur seals were heading toward extinction; and sea lions and harbor seals were on the decline, often shot by fisherman who didn't think much of the idea of sharing the ocean's bounty. Before the passage of the Marine Mammal Protection Act of 1972 harbor seals, sea lions, and other marine mammals were killed indiscriminately, and there were even government bounties to encourage the killing. It was easier to blame pinnipeds for the state's declining fisheries than to deal with the real sources of the problem: dams, pollution, overfishing, and clear-cutting, which clogs spawning streams with sediment.

The difference between seals and sea lions can best be seen in how they move about on land. Seals use their front flippers to drag themselves around on shore, their rear flippers dragging helplessly

WHERE TO SEE SEALS AND SEA LIONS:

1 Santa Catalina Island.
2 Channel Islands National Park.
3 Garrapata State Park.
4 Point Lobos State Reserve.
5 Santa Cruz.
6 Año Nuevo State Reserve.
7 California Marine Mammal Center.
8 Farallon Islands.
9 Point Reyes National Seashore.
10 Sonoma Coast State Beaches.
11 MacKerricher State Park.
12 Humboldt Bay National Wildlife Refuge.

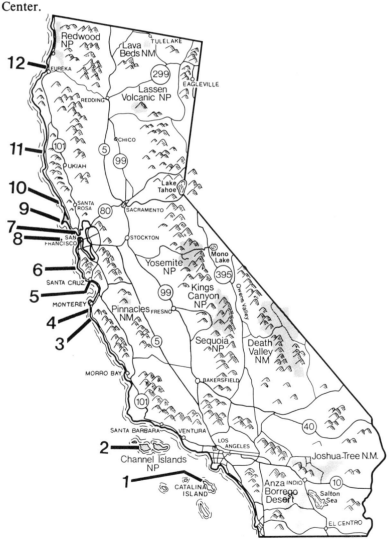

behind. Sea lions are much more mobile on land because their rear flippers pivot to the side to help them walk. Out of their element on land, seals and sea lions move about with a clumsy lack of grace. But in water they glide with the form and ease of birds through air.

California Sea Lions: These playful and intelligent trained "seals" of circuses, zoos, and seaquariums are really California sea lions. They are often seen lounging on rocks, where they can bark in unison for hours. Bulls weigh as much as 600 pounds and reach seven feet in length. Cows are generally a foot shorter and weigh only about 200 pounds. California sea lions are much smaller than their steller sea lion cousins. Pups are born between May and June.

Steller Sea Lions: Bulls of this species may weigh a ton and stretch eight feet in length. Cows are much smaller at seven feet and 600 pounds. During breeding season bulls form harems that may include a dozen females.

Elephant Seals: These are easily the most impressive, if not the most lovable, of California's pinnipeds. The world's largest seals, they may strike you as awesome, bazaar, and even grotesque. Males weigh up to 6,000 pounds and stretch as much as 18 feet in length. They are easily recognizable by their large bulbous proboscises, which are used for resonating their territorial claims. Females are only 11 feet long and weigh only 2,000 pounds. Spending most of their lives at sea, these giant mammals come ashore in late fall and winter to mate and bear young.

Harbor Seals: These pudgy, black-spotted fellows are often seen resting on the rocks and shores of the coast, especially in coves and estuaries. Harbor seals are curious about people, often approaching shore to stare at people staring back at them. These are the northern hemisphere's most common seals. They are also the smallest, reaching five feet in length, and weighing 255 pounds. Eating almost any kind of fish, mollusk, and crustacean, they even venture into freshwater after prey.

Seals and sea lions are seen in hundreds of places on the California coast; far too many to mention here. Generally, they are most often seen where there are offshore rocks for them to rest on, though they also rest under piers and frolic along sandy beaches. Here are only a few of the best places to see them:

Santa Catalina Island
TO GET THERE... commercial boat trips leave from San Pedro, Long Beach, and other Southern California ports. Additional information is provided below.

Seals and sea lions are seen on the shores and offshore rocks of this popular resort island. A three-hour boat cruise around the island leaves from Avalon at noon daily from mid-June through mid September. Tickets are available from the Catalina Sightseeing ticket offices and at the Catalina Cruises office on Transportation Dock; or call (313) 510-2628. The tour stops at Twin Harbors, where camping is allowed, at the picturesque west end of the island. Camping reservation may be made by contacting: Los Angeles County Department of Parks and Recreation, Island Plaza, Avalon, CA 90704; (213) 510-0688. Hotel accommodations are available at Avalon.

For more information about tourist services, contact: Catalina Island Chamber of Commerce, P.O. Box 217, Avalon, CA 90704; (213) 510-1520. See Los Angeles and Orange county yellow pages for passenger service to and from the island.

Channel Island National Park

TO GET THERE... commercial passenger service is available from several Southern California ports. Additional information is mentioned below.

This park includes five spectacular wilderness islands, an ideal visit for those who love the ocean and its life. The most popular time to visit is summer, when days are long and mild, though sometimes foggy. Fall and spring often have the best weather, though; and even winter has many calm and sunny days.

Year-around boat trips for campers and day users are provided by the park concessionaire: Island Packers, 1695 Anchors Way Drive, Ventura, CA 93003; (805) 642-1393. They make an effort to pass by areas of wildlife interest, and allow extra time for whale-watching between December and March. They also provide charter service for groups, including a "floating classroom" for school groups. Be sure to make reservations at least two weeks in advance. For information about other companies serving the islands, and for camping permits and other information, contact: Channel Islands National Park, 1901 Spinnaker Drive, Ventura, CA 93001; (805) 644-8262.

In 1972 these islands were included in the federal National Marine Sanctuary Program, largely to protect seals and sea lions, and they entered the national park system in 1980.

SAN MIGUEL ISLAND: The westernmost of the Channel Islands, this small and austere outpost of land is one of the world's most diversified seal and sea lion rookeries, including 15,000 California and Steller sea lions, northern fur seals, elephant seals, and harbor seals. You can watch them breed, bear young, and rest on the beaches and surf-pounded rocks, especially between April and June. This is also a haulout place for the endangered Guadelupe fur seals, and a great place to see sea birds. With water clarity allowing visibility as deep as 75 feet, it is not unusual to watch sea lions dart through the water catching fish.

Access to the island is limited to Cuyler Harbor, and camping and day use are allowed by permit from park headquarters. Island Packers offers special pinniped trips during the spring breeding period.

The mating and pupping season brings great numbers of sea lions to San Miguel Island.

ANACAPA ISLAND: These prominent islands of rock are home for sea lions and harbor seals, which are most often seen on the islands' north shores. This is also the only Pacific coast nesting site for brown pelicans north of Mexico. Campers must register at park headquarters and may only spend the night on the east island. Bring your own food, fuel, water, and shelter.

SANTA BARBARA ISLAND: This small rocky triangular island offers an abundance of seals and sea lions, including elephant seals in winter. Almost entirely surrounded by cliffs, viewers may look down on basking marine mammals, and see gray whales in late fall and winter. Camping is allowed near the rangers quarters by permit from park headquarters. Bring your own food, water, fuel, and shelter.

SANTA CRUZ ISLAND: The largest of the Channel Islands, Santa Cruz is administered by the Nature Conservancy, a non-profit conservation organization that offers naturalist-led outings and interpretive programs. For more information, contact: The Nature Conservancy, Santa Cruz Island Project, 735 State Street, Suite 201, Santa Barbara, CA 93101; (805) 962-9111.

Intelligent and gregarious, California sea lions are natural comedians.

Marine Mammal Rescue

If you find an injured or ill seal or sea lion on the Southern California coast contact the Alliance for Wildlife Rehabilitation and Education, (213) 769-8388. The alliance has more than 260 Southern California member groups, and will refer you to the nearest participating agency or veterinarian.

Sea World, (714) 222-6363, rehabilitates sick and injured marine mammals. This famous 40-acre aquatic park is in San Diego's Mission Bay. The rescue facilities are open to the pubic.

Marineland, (213) 377-1571, operates a Marine Animal Care Center that is open to the public with the admission price to the park. This popular seaquarium is on the Palos Verdes Peninsula, south of Los Angeles.

Garrapata State Park

TO GET THERE.. the Soberanes Trail begins 4.6 miles south of the entrance to Point Lobos on Highway 1. Look for a cypress grove at the trailhead.

Before reaching Soberanes Point you will probably hear the eternal barking of sea lions on the two large offshore rocks. Also look for sea otters.

Point Lobos State Reserve

TO GET THERE.. it's about three miles south of Carmel and ten miles south of Monterey on Highway 1.

The wild headlands and offshore rocks of this spectacular peninsula form one of the best places on the coast to see California and Steller sea lions, as well as sea otters, sea birds, and tidepools. Sea lions are particularly abundant on Sea Lion Rock. The early Spaniards called sea lions "sea wolves," and named this granite point "El Punto De Los Lobos Marinos" -- The Point Of The Sea Wolves.

See map on page 82,

Santa Cruz

There are several good places to see seals and sea lions at this seaside resort town. Look for sea lions resting on the Municipal Pier support beams. On the west side of town Point Santa Cruz makes a scenic turnoff from West Cliff Drive. The picturesque Mark Abbott Memorial Lighthouse stands on the peninsula, and the rocks offshore are a sure place to see sea lions.

Año Nuevo State Reserve

TO GET THERE... take New Years Creek Road off Highway 1 about 19 miles north of Santa Cruz.

Elephant seal bulls have enormous proboscises for proclaiming their territorial and mating claims. Listen for a deep, resonating, gutteral sound. Año Nuevo Island is in the background.

This is truly one of America's great marine wildlife sanctuaries. Harbor seals are common features on the rocks and waters, and sea lions are most evident by their everlasting chorus of barks from the island offshore; and even sea otters are beginning to be seen here. The birdlife is also impressive, and sea caves, sand dunes, and tidepools add up to a place worth exploring.

The reserve is most popular from December through March when a colony of elephant seals visits the island and peninsula for mating and bearing young. To protect these enormous mammals, and the people who come to see them, the reserve is open only through naturalist guided-tours at this time of year. The popularity of these seals is a genuine phenomenon, sometimes making it necessary to get tickets months in advance for tours. Whether it is because of their size, their strange appearance, or perhaps the ease with which they are approached, they are one of the most popular attractions on the central California coast. Park rangers and students from the University of California at Santa Cruz conduct tours of the reserve when elephant seals are here in their greatest numbers between December and March. As of this writing, tickets are available from Ticketron. Be sure to get your tickets as early as possible. For more information, call the state park office at (415) 879-0227.

Male elephant seals arrive in December to establish a breeding hierarchy, followed in January by females who join the harems of the dominant males. Male seals are enormous, reaching lengths of 18 feet and weighting three tons. Females are much smaller, at 1,200 to 2,000 pounds. Slaughtered for their oil-rich blubber, by 1892 less

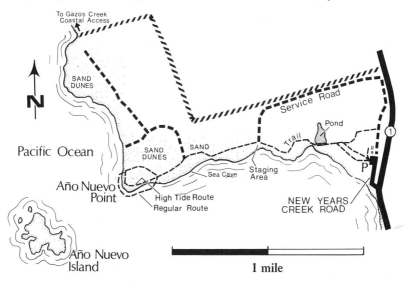

Female elephant seals resting on a beach.

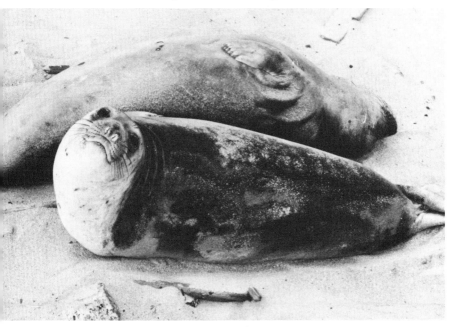

than 100 remained, mainly on the rugged shores of Guadalupe Island off Baja California. In the 1920's the Mexican and United States governments gave them legal protection, allowing their numbers to rapidly increase. In fact, biologists believe that all succeeding generations may be descended from one bull. This recovery is so spectacular that there is now concern that there will soon be too many of them. As they expand their range we will see how many beaches people are willing to share with giant seals.

Elephant seals first returned to Año Nuevo Island in 1955, and are now also breeding on the peninsula. The largest members of the seal family, they seem awkward on land; but they are excellent swimmers, able to dive as deep as 1,000 feet to feed mainly on rays, squid, skates, and fish.

This fascinating peninsula is worth exploring all year; and, in fact, may be most enjoyable when most of the elephant seals and their hordes of admirers are gone, and walking may be done without ranger escort. Sea lions, habor seals, and a few elephant seals, hang around all year.

Año Nuevo is one of the few places on the San Mateo County coast where it is possible to do some real hiking west from Highway 1. Follow the trail west from the parking area, passing a small marshy pond, sand dunes, and on to the tip of the peninsula, just over one mile from the parking lot. Half a mile off the peninsula is 12-acre Año Nuevo Island, breeding ground for elephant seals, California and Steller sea lions, and harbor seals; and a nesting place for western gulls, pigeon guillemots, and black oystercatchers. Because of its importance to wildlife, public access to the island is prohibited.

California Marine Mammal Center

TO GET THERE... from San Francisco, take Highway 101 across the Golden Gate Bridge to the first turnoff past the vista point. Turn left through the tunnel and on to Rodeo Lagoon.

This is a place to see both marine mammals and some of their most devoted human friends. On an abandoned missile site, the center is dedicated to the rescue, rehabilitation, and return to the wild of injured and sick seals and sea lions found on the Northern California coast from Monterey County to the Oregon border.

This private, non-profit center is not a zoo. These animals come from the wild, and with a lot of luck, and at least as much loving care, they will be back in their natural habitat as soon as possible. The Marine Mammal Center not only lets you see what it's doing, it

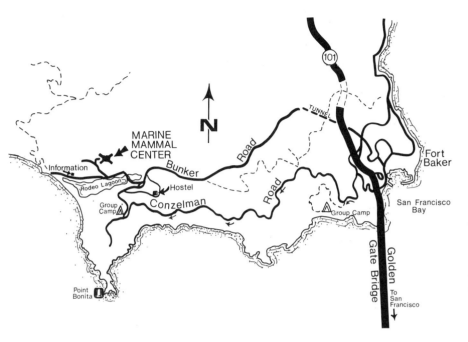

encourages you to visit and participate. The center is run by volunteers, supervised by a core of professionals, and is supported by membership dues, donations, and private grants. Volunteer docents will guide you around the facility, and you may buy something at the gift shop to help support the work.

The rescued animals suffer from a variety of ailments, parasites being a particularly common problem -- especially lungworm. Other mammals are injured, or wounded by people; some having been harassed by people and dogs on beaches where they were stranded. Elephant seals are admitted mainly as orphaned pups, and are nursed to health with a rich infant formula and force-feedings of whole fish. Unfortunately, the center is not yet equipped to handle dolphins and sea otters.

Marine mammal rehabilitation begins with establishing a network of concerned people along the coast. When an injured or diseased pinniped is sighted, a truck is dispatched to bring the patient to the Marin County facility for treatment, which may last several weeks, or a month or more. Volunteers are always needed.

If you find an injured or sick seal or sea lion, or would like to get involved with the center, call: (415) 331-SEAL.

Farallon Islands National Wildlife Preserve

TO GET THERE... the largest of the islands is 23 miles west of San Francisco. Boats are not allowed to land, but excursions to view island wildlife are conducted by The Oceanic Society (415) 441-1106, The Point Reyes Bird Observatory (415) 868-1221, The Golden Gate Chapter of the Audubon Society (415) 843-2222, and other organizations.

On clear days the largest of these eight barren, granite islands appear like floating castles on the western horizon. Though their combined land area is only about 211 acres, these rugged outposts of land are important rookeries for five species of seals and sea lions, including elephant seals. They are also nesting areas for cormorants, western gulls, murres, and other sea birds. In 1972 the federal government included the Farallons in the National Marine Sanctuary Program, largely to protect seals and sea lions.

The reduction of human disturbance has resulted in a dramatic increase in the numbers of birds and marine mammals visiting and breeding on the islands. In 1972 elephant seals returned for the first time in 60 years to mate and bear young; and since that year the sea lion population has exploded from 400 to 2,500. Because of the fragile ecology, the Point Reyes Bird Observatory, which administers the islands, allows only a few people each year -- mostly scientists -- to land. If you take a boat excursion past the islands be sure to bring binoculars, and be prepared for cold winds and rough seas. For more information, call the U.S. Fish and Wildlife Service at (415) 792-0222.

Point Reyes National Seashore

TO GET THERE... it's in Marin County, about 35 miles north of San Francisco. Take Highway 101 to the Sausalito turnoff on Highway 1, which goes west and north to the park; or take Highway 101 to San Rafael and head west on Sir Francis Drake Highway.

This 65,303-acre national seashore is a peninsula that is being torn away from the continent by the San Andreas Fault. It is a wild land of bays, estuaries, sandy beaches, and rocky headlands; and it is filled with marine and terrestrial wildlife, including seals and sea lions.

POINT REYES HEADLANDS: At the end of Sir Francis Drake Highway, the peninsula culminates at the majestic headlands sighted on January 6, 1603 by Sebastian Vizcaino and named "Punta de los Reyes" (Point of the Kings). These granite promontories plunge over high cliffs and into the PointReyes Headlands Research Natural Area, a virtually inaccessible rocky intertidal zone home to sea lions and California murres. The area is "set aside to protect and preserve coastal forms of life."

TOMALES POINT: This wild and scenic peninsula is at the north end of Pierce PointRoad, near McClures Beach. The isolated rocky sea shelves and beaches are ideal for seal and sea lion watching. Sometimes sea lions play in the churning surf at the end of the point.

See map on page 120.

Sonoma Coast State Beaches
TO GET THERE... this public coast stretches from just north of Bodega Bay to the Russian River. Take State Park Road west from Highway 1 to Goat Rock Beach, just south of the river's mouth.

Where the Russian River flows into the ocean, harbor seals can

---

Harbor seals are a common sight along California's coast, and are often as curious of people as we are of them. They prefer sheltered coves, bays, and river mouths.

often be seen by the dozens catching their meals where migrating fish funnel in and out of the river. These plump, spotted mammals are intelligent and alert when they aren't sleeping, and are sometimes seen more than half a mile up the river in totally fresh water. Harbor seals are sometimes kept in freshwater in captivity with no ill effects.

This beach has a wonderful display of seacoast features, including a river mouth, a sand bar, dunes, cliffs, and dramatic pinnacles of rock thrusting out of the ocean just offshore. it is also a good place to see pelicans, especially in summer.

MacKerricher State Park

TO GET THERE... it is three miles north of Fort Bragg on the Mendocino coast.

A herd of harbor seals live off this stretch of coast, and are often seen lounging on the rocks offshore. Sea lions are also seen. Camping is allowed.

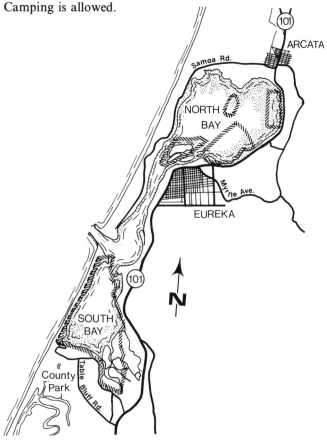

Humboldt Bay National Wildlife Refuge

TO GET THERE... take highway 101 from Eureka south to Hookton Road, which parallels the refuge and continues south to the south spit.

This 8,600-acre preserve is popular with waterfowl, shore and marsh birds, and harbor seals, who live here by the hundreds and bear their pups in the refuge.

Wildlife Photography

Photography enhances many of the skills used in wildlife watching. In the act of taking pictures the senses are attuned and an aesthetic perception is developed. The process of taking the picture is often more important than the photographic image itself.

It is helpful to know something about the behavior of the animals you wish to photograph, including what they eat, where they are most likely to be found, and what time of the day or night they are active. With this knowledge you will know when and how to get the most exciting shots.

Because wild animals rarely cooperate with your efforts to photograph them, the ability to watch, wait, and listen are essential qualities for successful wildlife photography. It is also important that patience be coupled with alertness and quick reflexes. At Año Nuevo one winter day all the elephant seals seemed to be taking a siesta, so after taking a few pictures I put my camera back in its case. Suddenly a belligerant bull raised his massive head, bellowed out a gutteral roar, and charged at a rival seal. Needless to say, I lost a great action shot. Bobcats, cougars, eagles, and other wildlife usually appear for a fleeting glimpse, and will be photographed only if you are ready. Professionals insist that the best way to get really good results is to use lots of film and to keep only the best shots. To get more photos in less time a motor-drive attachment is useful.

The best camera to use is a 35mm single-lens reflex. They are light and portable, and allow for easy lens changes. A longer lens, between 135mm and 400mm is nearly essential for serious photographers. Without some magnification the animals you photograph will often be hardly recognizable on the final print or slide. A long lens also prevents unnecessary disturbance of the subject by making it possible to get good pictures from a respectable distance.

Tidepools

and the intertidal zone.

BETWEEN PACIFIC TIDES is a narrow zone where marine life may be more abundant and varied than anywhere else. Where pools of the ocean are left behind in rocky basins by the receding tide you will find microcosms of the sea, natural aquariums for sea stars, sea anemones, sea urchins, hermits crabs, chitons, and a cornucopia of other strange and wonderful creatures. Once you get into tide-pooling, sandy beaches may seem boring by comparison.

The best time to go is when the tide is low. Check the newspaper, or better, get a tide table; usually available from sporting good stores. The best tidepooling is when the tide is indicated with a minus symbol. Be sure to be on the coast at least an hour before low tide, to ensure the most time for exploring. A ten-power magnifying glass will be invaluable for examing what you find, and a copy of *Between Pacific Tides* (Ricketts and Calvin, Stanford Press) will help to identify specimens.

There are a lot of opportunities for getting hurt around tide-pools, so make safety a top priority. Wear rough rubber-soled shoes for traction on slippery rocks and seaweed; and never turn your back to the ocean when near the water. An unexpectedly large wave could drench you, or even wash you away.

SOME OF THE BEST TIDEPOOLING PLACES:

1 Cabrillo National Monument.
2 La Jolla Underwater Park.
3 Scripps Institution of Oceanography
4 Dana Point Harbor.
5 Laguna Beach Ecological Reserve.
6 Santa Catalina Island.
7 Palos Verdes Peninsula.
8 Cabrillo Museum.
9 Channel Islands National Park.

10 Point Dume State Park.
11 Carpinteria State Beach.
12 Point Sal State Beach.
13 Montana De Oro State Park.
14 Point Lobos State Reserve.
15 Carmel River State Beach.
16 Natural Bridges State Park.
17 Pebble Beach State Park.
18 Pigeon Point.
19 James Fitzgerald Marine Reserve.
20 Agate Beach County Park.
21 Point Reyes National Seashore.
22 Bodega Head State Park.
23 Salt Point State Park.
24 Mendocino Headlands State Park.
25 Trinidad State Beach.

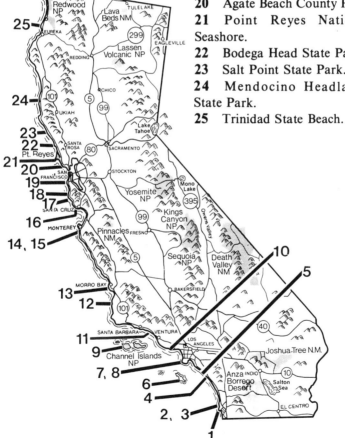

The most important rule of tidepooling is to put back whatever you pick up. Many formerly bountiful tidepools have been denuded of life by thoughtless visitors who want to take home every interesting thing they find, sometimes even using buckets to speed up the process. Many people have the misconception that a new batch of marine life will wash in with the next tide. This is not true. Many of the animals that are removed make their permanent homes in these rocky pools.

There are tidepools along the entire 1,100-mile coast of California. The best ones tend to be in remote places, usually in the northern part of the state, where people haven't kidnapped tidepool inhabitants. With milder water temperatures, however, Southern California has the advantage in snorkeling, which is the best way to explore shallow clear waters. This sport is only for good swimmers and is best in calm, protected coves where waves don't stir up the bottom sand and debris.

Here are just a few of some of California's best tidepooling places, ranging from south to north:

Cabrillo National Monument
TO GET THERE... on Point Loma, take Catalina Boulevard ten miles south from San Diego.

Ranger-led tidepool walks are conducted at low tide. This is also a good place for whale-watching in winter. For information, call (714) 293-5450.

See map on page 115.

Bird Rock
TO GET THERE... from La Jolla, take La Jolla Boulevard south and turn west on Bird Rock Avenue to the coast, south of the Scripps Institute.

There are some good tidepools on this rocky stretch of coast.

La Jolla Underwater Park
TO GET THERE... it's off La Jolla Boulevard, near downtown La Jolla and the Scripps Institute.

At La Jolla Cove, this preserve has abundant submarine and intertidal life in what is called La Jolla Canyon. Buoys and shore markers identify the reserve for snorkelers. Underwater visibility here is exceptional.

Scripps Institution of Oceanography
TO GET THERE... take La Jolla Shores Drive in La Jolla.

The Thomas Wayland Vaughan aquarium-museum has a working tidepool model that will help you learn about marine ecology. This live exhibit of deep water and tidepool life makes learning a pleasure. It is open from 9 a.m. to 5 p.m. and has no admission fee.

Palos Verdes Peninsula

TO GET THERE.. it can be reached by way of routes 107 and 11 south of Los Angeles. Palos Verdes Drive follows the coast. Abalone Cove, just east of Marineland, is the best snorkeling, and one of the best tidepooling spots in the Los Angeles area. With visibility up to 15 feet, sea urchins, anemones, and fish are among animals easily seen through the calm, shallow water.

The Cabrillo Museum

TO GET THERE... take Highway 11 south from Los Angeles to where it ends in San Pedro. Turn left on Gaffey Street and left on 22nd Street, right on Pacific Avenue, and left on 36th Street, which becomes Stephen White Drive. The museum is at 3720 Stephen White Drive, San Pedro, CA 90731. Here you will find 30 aquariums for getting acquainted with Southern California marine life. Displays depict rocky shorelines, sandy beaches, mudflats, and open ocean. There is also a gray whale skeleton. It is open from noon to 5 p.m. on weekends.

Santa Catalina Island

TO GET THERE...commercial passenger service is available from San Pedro, Long Beach, and other Southern California ports. Additional information is provided below. The 55 miles of rocky shoreline of this popular resort island have many excellent tidepools, and the water is extraordinarily clear and calm. This clearness extends tidepooling to new depths and allows the eye to probe deeper than the lowest minus tide. There is good tidepooling and snorkeling near Two Harbors, where camping is permitted. For campsite reservations, contact: Los Angeles County Department of Parks and Recreation, Island Plaza, Avalon, CA 90704; (213) 510-0688.

The underwater preserve at Lovers Cove, southeast of Steamship Dock, is good for snorkeling and fish-watching. Forty-minute glass bottom boat tours operate year around.

You might also want to take the one-hour flying fish boat tour from June through September. These evening excursions use a powerful searchlight to scan the water for the famous fish that soar out of the water and sometimes land in the boat.

The Catalina Island Marine Institute, Box 796, Toyon Bay, Avalon, CA 90704, has study programs of tidepools, ecology, geology, and other natural features. The Institute is in a Spanish-style building two miles up the coast from Avalon.

Boat transit to the island is available from several companies. Check the yellow pages for Los Angeles and Orange counties or contact the Visitors Information and Services Center, Box 737, Avalon, CA 90704; or call (213) 510-2500. Two of the main passenger carriers are: Catalina Express, Box 1391, San Pedro, CA 90733, (213) 519-1212; and, Catalina Cruises, Box 1948-CC, San Pedro, CA 90733, (213)

See map on page 88.

Channel Islands National Park

TO GET THERE... commercial passenger service is available from Ventura, San Pedro, and other Southern California ports. Several companies are listed below.

The five wilderness islands of this park are alive with seals and sea lions, birds, and some of the most bountiful and undisturbed tidepool areas in the state. The water is wonderfully clear, because of the absence of major streams that emit sediment into the ocean, and you can peer deep into the pools and snorkel in some of the sheltered inlets. Summer is the most popular time to visit because of the long days and lack of rain, though some days are foggy. The islands offer more solitude in spring and fall, and even winter has many mild and sunny days. Water clarity is at its best in early fall, when the weather and the water are most calm.

Commercial boat service is available from many Southern California ports. For further information, contact: Channel Islands National Park, 1901 Spinnaker Drive, Ventura, CA 93001; (805) 644-8262. Year-round boat trips for campers and day users are provided by: Island Packers, 1695 Anchors Way Drive, Ventura, CA 93003; (805) 642-1393. They make an effort to pass by areas of wildlife interest, and allow extra time for whale-watching between December and March. They also provide charter service for groups, including a "floating classroom" for school groups.

ANACAPA ISLAND: These small craggy islands sit on the ocean like rock-hewn ships, forming an ideal habitat for seals, sea lions, a multitude of birds, and a wonderland for snorkelers. Campers must register at park headquarters and may only stay on the east island.

The west island is protected as a brown pelican rookery, but you may visit it during the day. Here you may explore Frenchy's Cove, with underwater visibility of 50 feet in summer for outstanding snorkeling and skindiving, though there aren't many accessible tidepools. Landing on the islands is allowed only with written permission of the park superintendent.

SAN MIGUEL ISLAND: The rocky shelves of this wave-battered island hold many tidepools. An abundance of birds, seals, and sea lions are also seen here, on the westernmost of the Channel Islands.

SANTA BARBARA ISLAND: The rocky shores of this small island offer nearly pristine tidepools, along with sea caves, blowholes, and a host of birds, seals, and sea lions. Camping is allowed near the ranger's quarters by permit from park headquarters. Bring food, water, fuel, and shelter.

SANTA CRUZ ISLAND: This large wilderness island is owned by The Nature Conservancy, a non-profit conservation organization. For information about naturalist-led day trips, contact them at: Santa Cruz Island Project, 735 State Street, Suite 201, Santa Barbara, CA 93101; (805) 962-9111.

See map on page 88.

Leo Carrillo Beach State Park
TO GET THERE... go 12 miles west from Malibu on the Coast Highway.

Here you will find a combination of sandy beaches and rocky tidepool areas.

Laguna Beach Ecological Reserve
TO GET THERE... in Laguna Beach, it is at the city park on Cliff Drive.

This reserve has three excellent snorkeling areas with good underwater visibility in summer and fall.

Point Dume Beach State Park
TO GET THERE... in Los Angeles County, go eight miles west of Malibu on Highway 1.

This sandstone peninsula is a good place to see sea birds and tidepools.

Carpinteria State Beach
TO GET THERE... in the town of Carpinteria, drive 12 miles south of Santa Barbara.

This park offers ranger-led tidepool walks. For more information, call (805) 684-2811.

A few of the intertidal creatures you may see:

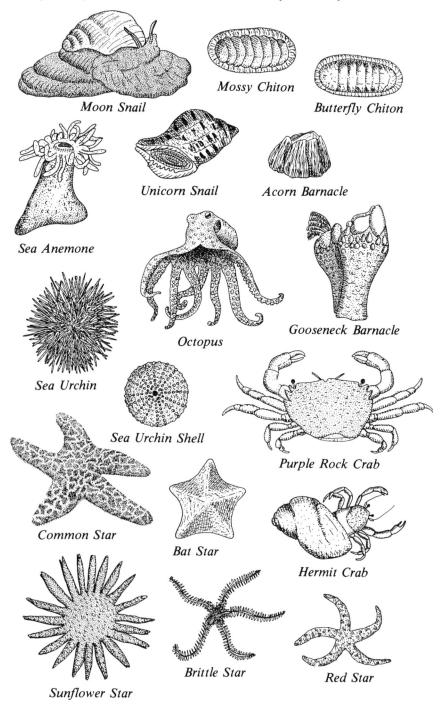

Moon Snail

Mossy Chiton

Butterfly Chiton

Sea Anemone

Unicorn Snail

Acorn Barnacle

Octopus

Gooseneck Barnacle

Sea Urchin

Sea Urchin Shell

Purple Rock Crab

Common Star

Bat Star

Hermit Crab

Sunflower Star

Brittle Star

Red Star

Point Sal State Beach

TO GET THERE... take Brown Road nine miles west from Highway 1, south of Guadalupe. It is in northern Santa Barbara County.

This is one of the most fertile intertidal areas in the state, with rocks that are packed with sea anemones, mussels, chitons, barnacles, and especially sea stars. There is also a sandy beach. The last part of the road access is dirt and may not be passable in wet weather.

Montana De Oro State Park

TO GET THERE... take Pecho Road seven miles south of Los Osos.

There are good tidepools at Spooner Cove, Hazard Reef, and Coralina Cove. Camping facilities are provided.

Point Lobos State Reserve

TO GET THERE... it's about three miles south of Carmel and 10 miles south of Monterey on Highway 1.

The water of this peninsula's coves and pools is extraordinarily clear, like natural aquariums, helping to make this one of the best tidepooling spots on the central coast. All marine life is strictly protected both on shore and in the 755-acre marine reserve offshore from the peninsula. Ranger-led tidepool walks are worth attending even at dawn, or whenever else the tide is low. Also look for sea otters, seals, and sea lions here. For more information, call (408) 624-4909.

See map on page 82,

Carmel River State Beach

TO GET THERE... look for the beach just off Highway 1 between Carmel and Point Lobos.

This calm and protected part of Carmel Bay is one of the region's most popular diving spots.

Monterey Peninsula

This granite-clad peninsula exposes many tidepools when the tide goes out. You can also take glass bottom boat tours over the Pacific Grove Marine Gardens off Point Aulon on calm summer days. The water here is unusually clear and abounds with marine life. Its rugged sea bottom enhances the garden's ecology by providing habitat for various animals and by helping to mix surface and bottom waters. At Point Cabrillo, Stanford University operates the Hopkins Marine Station, specializing in the study of intertidal ecology. For more information, contact: (408) 373-0464.

See map on page 83.

Natural Bridges State Park
TO GET THERE... in Santa Cruz, take Mission Street to the park.
This park has tidepools and interpretive walks led by rangers and students from U.C. Santa Cruz. For more information, call (408) 423-4609. The University of California at Santa Cruz has a small aquarium at the Long Marine Laboratory next to Natural Bridges. Free tours of the facility include tanks containing local specimens and a gray whale skeleton. For more information, call (408) 429-4087.

Pebble Beach State Park
TO GET THERE... in San Mateo County, drive 18 miles south of Half Moon Bay on Highway 1.
Tidepools are found on both sides of the beach.

Pigeon Point
TO GET THERE... in southern San Mateo County, look for the lighthouse on Highway 1 between Half Moon Bay and Santa Cruz.
There are outstanding tidepools just north of the lighthouse.

The Fitzgerald Marine Reserve
TO GET THERE... take Highway 1 about seven miles north from Half Moon Bay. It's between Princeton Beach and Moss Beach.
This large, rocky reef is one of the largest and most popular tidepool areas on this part of the coast. This area has been stripped of marine life in the past, and it is now strictly protected. For information on naturalist-led interpretive walks, call (415) 728-3584.

Steinhart Aquarium
TO GET THERE... it's at the California Academy of Sciences in San Francisco's Golden Gate Park.
Here you will find a working tidepool replica inhabited by a wide range of intertidal life.

Agate Beach County Park
TO GET THERE... in the town of Bolinas, in Marin County, take Elm Street west to the coast.
Here is Duxbury Reef, a large rock shelf that forms one of the state's biggest and most popular tidepool areas.

Point Reyes National Seashore
TO GET THERE... it's in Marin County, about 35 miles north of San Francisco. Take Highway 101 to the Sausalito turnoff on Highway 1, which goes west and north to the park; or take Highway 101 to San Rafael and head west on Sir Francis Drake Highway.

This large triangular-shaped peninsula has many tidepools. One of the best is Palomarin Beach, which is four miles north of Bolinas on Mesa Road. More tidepools are found at McClures Beach, at the north end of Pierce Point Road.

See map on page 120.

Bodega Head State Park
TO GET THERE... from the town of Bodega Bay take Bay Flat Road west.

These rugged, granite headlands, exposed to the full force of Pacific wind and waves, have lots of unspoiled tidepools to explore. Camping is at Bodega Dunes Campground, half a mile north of Bodega Bay.

Trinidad State Beach
TO GET THERE... this beach is 19 miles north of Eureka on Highway 101.

From the town of Trinidad, follow the signs to Humboldt State University Marine Laboratory, where a three-quarter mile trail goes to several good tidepool areas.

Salt Point State Park
TO GET THERE... in Sonoma County, take Highway 1 between Jenner and Stewarts Point.

This is one of California's best tidepooling and diving spots.

Mendocino Headlands State Park
TO GET THERE... it's at the mouth of the Big River, near Mendocino.

This whole stretch of coast has a galaxy of tidepools.

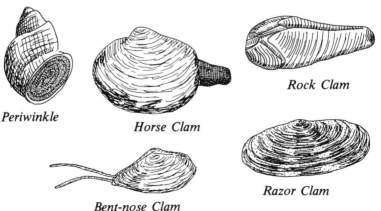

Periwinkle

Horse Clam

Rock Clam

Bent-nose Clam

Razor Clam

Whales

WHALES LIVE AT the interface between water and air. They live in the water, yet must always be close enough to the surface to come up for air. This makes them mysterious and awesome; large shadowy forms that break through the surface and then are gone. Whale-watching requires a healthy imagination to compensate for what we can't see from the surface.

Each winter hundreds of thousands of Californians gather on coastal overlooks and cruise the coastal waters in boats to watch gray whales make their way down the shoreline. This is truly one of the grandest and most exciting wildlife displays to be seen anywhere.

Once there were three populations of gray whales in the world: the western Pacific (near Japan), the northern Atlantic, and our whales on the west coast of North America. Centuries of slaughter for whale oil drove the first two into extinction, and the California grays would have joined them if not for conservationists in the United States and Mexico. Of an original population of perhaps fifteen thousand, fewer than 100 were recorded on their southward migration in 1937. Their fate seemed dim when multi-nation protection laws were enacted in 1947, and since then their numbers have increased to a current population of just over ten thousand whales.

WHERE TO SEE WHALES:

1 Cabrillo National Monument
2 Point La Jolla.
3 The Palos Verdes Peninsula.
4 Channel Islands National Park.
5 Point Dume State Park.
6 Jalama Beach County Park.
7 The Big Sur Coast.
8 Garrapata State Park.
9 Point Lobos State Reserve.
10 Monterey Peninsula.
11 San Mateo County Coast.
12 Farallon Islands.
13 Point Reyes National Seashore.
14 Bodega Head State Park.
15 Manchester State Park.
16 Humboldt Bay Area.

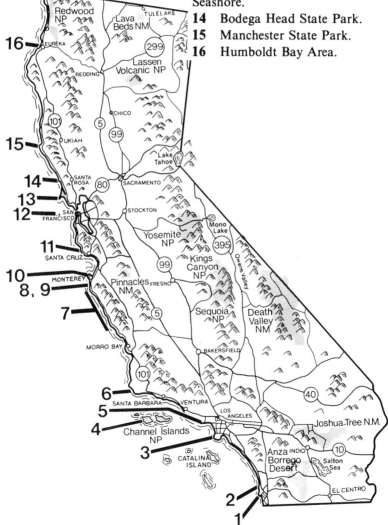

This remarkable recovery offers hope for other species of whales now approaching extinction.

California gray whales generally reach lengths of 40 feet or more and commonly weigh about 40 tons. Instead of teeth, they feed by straining ocean water through stiff cartilage called baleen. These giant mammals are a mottled gray color, though they usually also have light patches created by the largest barnacle accumulations found on any whale. They are one of the few whale species lacking a dorsal fin.

Whales and dolphins belong to the order of cetaceans, which have dwelled in the oceans for close to sixty million years. Their ancient ancestors lived on land, and their skeletons still show remnants of their terrestrial heritage. Their flipper bones bear an amazing resemblance to our hands, with five jointed fingers; and small remnant pelvic bones are vestiges of a time when they had hind limbs for walking on land.

Gray whales spend their summers in Alaskan waters gorging on small crustaceans called amphipods. Bottom feeders, they swim on their sides just above the ocean floor, sucking in water and sediments and straining out the edibles with their 150 baleen plates.

The gray whale migration--from their arctic feeding areas to their calving and breeding waters in several sheltered bays in Baja California—is the longest migration of any mammal, covering about 10,000 miles during their eight month round trip. They travel an amazing 80 to 100 miles per day, and eat little if any food on their

Watch for these whale maneuvers:

Spy-hopping

Peeking

Throwing Fluke

Breaching

Diving

journey because thick layers of blubber developed in the chilly Alaskan waters nourish them in the southern latitudes where they don't need as much insulation. This long fast costs them about 20 to 30 per cent of their body weight. Whale navigation is still a mystery, though it seems that they find their way down the coast by identifying submarine and surface features.

In March and April you may see whales off our coast again--this time heading north. This return to Alaska is for some reason more leisurely--perhaps because they are now traveling with newborn calves--allowing viewers to watch individual whales for longer periods. The problem for whale-watchers is that they travel farther offshore on their northward trek and are not seen as often from land.

Gray whales are a common sight along California's eleven hundred miles of coast, and can be seen from a lot more places than I have space to mention here. The best viewing spots are high ground, especially on peninsulas, where you can see out over the ocean. Scan the surface for moving gray humps and small clouds of mist; and then focus your binoculars on that area. Typically three to five successive spouts precede a dive, which may be more than 100 feet deep and cover a thousand feet of horizontal distance in three to five

minutes. Generally, the more times they spout the longer they stay submerged. A little experience will make you an expert on anticipating where they will surface. At a normal cruising speed of only four miles per hour, whales are fairly easy to track.

Whales' backs and flukes are usually all you see, but lucky whale-gazers sometimes see whales raising their heads above the water to look around--a practice called "spy-hopping." Even more unusual is a spectacular burst out of the water called "breaching," which seems to be done just for fun. If you see three whales together you may be witnessing the mating ceremony, which usually consists of a male, a female, and a male consort. Mating is often followed by a spectacular dive, with flukes flinging up water and fins flailing about with exuberance. After a gestation period of 13 months, pregnant females give birth to calves that are close to 16 feet long.

Whale-watching is best from December through February, though they are sometimes seen swimming south as early as November and as late as April for their northward return. My experience is that January is the best month. Though this is our stormiest month, you will find sunny, and even mildly warm periods just right for a day at the coast.

Gray whales aren't the only cetaceans living near our coast. White-sided dolphins are still common, especially in Southern California waters; and the endangered blue and finback whales still occasionally pass through our stretch of the Pacific. The return of the humpback whales is particularly exciting. About 300 of these great whales swim along our coast, heading south in fall, and back north in spring; and an increasing number seem to be making their permanent homes in the waters off the Farallon Islands, west of San Francisco.

Here are some of the best places to see whales, from south to north:

Cabrillo National Monument
TO GET THERE... take Cabrillo Memorial Drive south from San Diego, on Point Loma.

This is one of the state's most popular whale-watching spots. Don't miss the Whale Overlook, about 100 yards south of the old Point Loma Lighthouse via a footpath. Look for 70 to 80 whales a day spouting just beyond the kelp beds in mid-January. Ranger talks and tape-recorded messages explain the migration. You can also watch them from the restored lantern room in the old lighthouse, which was built in 1855.

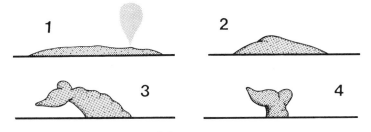

Normal diving sequence.

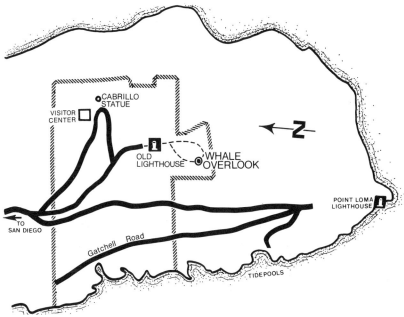

Point La Jolla

TO GET THERE... in La Jolla, take Coast Boulevard north from **Prospect Street.**

The configuration of land and underwater rocks bring whales close to shore here.

Channel Islands National Park

TO GET THERE... Commercial boat service is available from Ventura, San Pedro, and other Southern California Ports. Several carriers are listed below. For additional information contact park headquarters in Ventura.

The Channel Islands have many wonderful scenic promontories for viewing the annual whale parade. Anacapa Island seems especially good. From the East End Landing, take the 153 steps to the island's plateau, which has nearly two miles of nature trails and views of the ocean. Camping is allowed on Anacapa and Santa Barbara islands with a free permit from park headquarters, at 1901 Spinnaker Drive, Ventura, CA 93001; or call (805) 644-8262. Access to privately owned Santa Cruz Island may be arranged with the Nature Conservancy, Santa Cruz Island Project, 735 State Street, Suite 201, Santa Barbara, CA 93101; (805) 962-9111.

Whales are also often seen on the way to and from the islands by boat. Most companies serving the islands move in close to get a look at the passing cetaceans. Naturalist-led "floating classrooms" are available with Island Packers for those wanting to learn more about marine ecology. Also keep an eye open for white-sided dolphins. For reservations and information, contact: Island Packers, 1695 Anchors way Drive, Ventura, CA 93001; (805) 642-1303. Check the yellow pages for Los Angeles and Orange counties for other companies offering service.

See map on page 88

This photo was taken from East Anacapa, looking west toward Middle Anacapa and West Anacapa. This island has high overlooks, ideal for watching whales.

The Palos Verdes Peninsula
TO GET THERE... south of Los Angeles, this peninsula may be reached via Highway 107 and Highway 11 (to San Pedro). Palos Verdes Drive parallels the coast.

This stretch of coast has the best whale-watching in the Los Angeles area. A good place to look is from near the Point Fermin lighthouse at Point Fermin Park, on Paseo Del Mar, in San Pedro.

Jalama Beach County Park
TO GET THERE... take Highway 1 south from Lompoc, and head south and west on Jalama Road.

This beautiful and fairly isolated stretch of coast is good for seeing whales, seals, sea lions, and for tidepooling. It's about five miles from Point Conception, one of the most prominent points on the coast, which is accessible at low tide. For camping and other information, call: (805) 734-1446.

The Big Sur Area
TO GET THERE... on Highway 1, it is between Monterey and San Simeon.

There are many high overlooks where whales are seen along Highway 1. At Julia Pfeifer Burns State Park there is a spectacular trail that passes views of a waterfall and ends at a whale-watching overlook.

Garrapata State Park
TO GET THERE... the Soberanes Trail begins 4.6 miles south of the entrance to PointLobos on Highway 1. Look for a cypress grove at the trailhead.

Whales are seen from Soberanes Point, which can be reached via an easy 1.2 mile trail from Highway 1. This new trail will eventually continue for four miles to the beach at Garrapata Creek. For updated information, call park headquarters at (408) 667-2315.

Point Lobos State Reserve
TO GET THERE... it's about three miles south of Carmel on Highway 1.

Whales and other marine mammals are often seen from granite overlooks, especially from the trail near North Point. Portuguese whalers hunted gray whales here between 1861 and 1884, and hauled their catches to the protected waters of Whalers Cove, near park headquarters.
See map on page 82

Monterey Peninsula

Look for whales from the 17-Mile Drive, between Pacific Grove and Carmel.

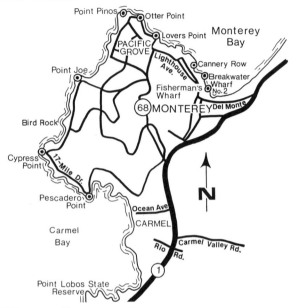

San Mateo County Coast

Whales are seen from the cliff highlands on Highway 1 between Pacifica and Davenport, and at Pigeon Point (near the lighthouse), south of Half Moon Bay.

Farallon Islands National Wildlife Preserve

TO GET THERE... the islands begin 23 miles west of San Francisco. Boats are not allowed to land on these rocks, but excursions to view island wildlife are conducted by The Oceanic Society (415) 441-1106, The Point Reyes Bird Observatory (415) 868-1221, The Golden Gate Chapter of the Audubon Society (415) 843-2222, and other organizations. Other companies offering boat trips are listed in Bay Area yellow pages under "fishing parties."

The rough, nutrient-rich waters off the Farallon Islands are witnessing the amazing homecoming of the humpback whales. These 50-foot marine giants, characterized by long, white flippers, are not really humpbacked at all, but get their name from the habit of exposing large parts of their backs when they dive.

Humpbacks were common in California waters in the nineteenth century, and were exterminated by whalers until as recently as

1966, when they were granted protection by the International Whaling Commission. There are now only 1,000 of these great whales left in the Pacific, and only 7,000 in the world. Their numbers are increasing, though, and in 1980 an important discovery was made: humpbacks have returned in significant numbers to the waters near the Farallon Islands, one of their ancestral feeding and breeding areas. As many as 65 of these whales have been seen together--including bulls, cows, and newborn calves--and it is not known how many more there are.

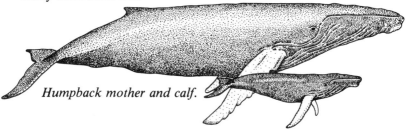

Humpback mother and calf.

Ocean currents join with nutrient-rich upwelling waters in the Farallon Basin to produce an area that is teeming with life. Humpbacks feed on the abundant schools of small fish and crustaceans, which also support large numbers of seals, sea lions, birds, and dolphins.

August and September seem to be the best months to see humpbacks. That's when they are most common, and it is also when the often foggy skies are most clear and the notoriously rough seas are most tranquil.

Point Reyes National Seashore

TO GET THERE... it's in Marin County, about 35 miles north of San Francisco. Take Highway 101 to the Sausalito turnoff on Highway 1, which goes west and north to the park; or take Highway 101 to San Rafael and head west on Sir Francis Drake Highway.

The area around the Point Reyes Lighthouse is one of the best, and most popular whale-watching places in the state. The lofty Point Reyes headlands provide an excellent view of the deep Pacific waters, just a few hundred yards offshore, where whales are often seen spouting. Whale-watching has become so popular that the park provides free shuttle bus service between Drakes Beach and the lighthouse.

To reach the lighthouse you must walk the 429 steps down the face of the cliff to its spectacular perch over the ocean. Don't miss the lighthouse itself, a fine-crafted piece of brass machinery assembled in Paris in 1867, and placed here in 1870. The ultimate in light technology, it wasn't replaced by an automated signal until 1975, when it opened to the public. The prism lense contains over a thousand pieces of glass, enabling the light of four oil-burning wicks to be seen for 24 nautical miles out to sea. It's open from 10 a.m. to 4:30 p.m. daily except Tuesdays and Wednesdays, or when winds exceed 40 miles per hour.

The steep headlands overlooking Chimney Rock, south of the lighthouse, are also good for whale-watching, and are a lot less crowded than the lighthouse.

There are many other places at the national seashore for seeing whales. Tomales Point, a scenic walk north from the end of Pierce Point Road, is one.

Point Reyes National Seashore is a triangular chunk of land ripped away from the Marin County mainland by the San Andreas Fault to form a separate and a diverse land with a unique history, ecology, and scenery. Its high overlooks and westward thrust makes it an ideal place to watch the gray whale migration.

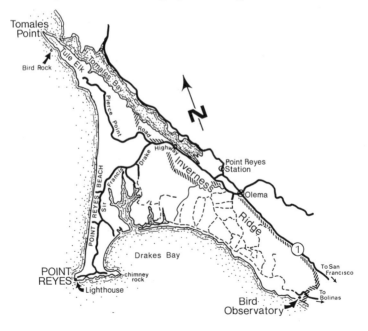

The author watching whales from the Point Reyes headlands.

Bodega Head State Park
TO GET THERE... from the town of Bodega Bay take Bay Flat Road west.

This rugged granite promontory sticks far enough into the ocean and high enough above the water to provide good views of migrating gray whales. Camping is allowed at Bodega Dunes Campground, half a mile north of Bodega Bay.

Sonoma and Mendocino Counties
North from Bodega Bay Highway 1 hugs the spectacular rocky coast through Sonoma and Mendocino counties, offering countless opportunities to watch migrating whales. Camping along this stretch of coast is allowed at Sonoma Coast, Salt Point, Manchester, Van Damme, Russian Gulch, and MacKerricher state parks.

Humboldt Bay Area
Whales can be seen from Table Bluff County Park, near Eureka, which has a sweeping panorama of the ocean to the west.

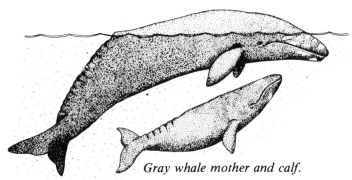
Gray whale mother and calf.

BOAT TOURS

The closest you can get to whales without getting wet is by boat. There are many companies that will take you right up to the gentle giants, usually from a few hours to half a day. The disadvantages are that you will probably have to make reservations a week or two ahead, pay your money, and risk poor weather, or and absence of whales. Most whale tour boats are charter fishing boats most of the year; so look in the yellow pages under "fishing parties." From south to north, here are the main ports for whale cruises:

Oceanside	Ventura
San Diego	Santa Barbara
Mission Bay	Morro Bay
Dana Point	Monterey
Balboa	Half Moon Bay
San Pedro	Princeton Beach
Long Beach	San Francisco
Redondo Beach	Sausalito
Marina Del Rey	Bodega Bay

The following organizations offer naturalist-led whale trips:
- Island Packers, 1695 Anchors Way Drive, Ventura, CA 93001; (805) 642-1393.
- Oceanic Society, Building 315, Fort Mason, San Francisco, CA 94123; (415) 775-6880.
- The Lawrence Hall Of Science, U.C. Berkeley, 94720; (415) 642-5132.
- Nature Explorations--Tuleyome, 2253Park Boulevard, Palo Alto, CA 94306; (415) 324-8737.
- The American Cetacean Society, Box 4416, San Pedro, CA 90731; (213) 548-6279.

Other Wildlife

THERE ARE MANY mammals, birds, mollusks, insects, and other classifications of animal life you are likely to run into, though hopefully not over, while exploring this state. Bookstores and libraries carry many excellent field guides to help you become familiar with these and other life forms. The following mammals are not concentrated in specific places where they can be easily seen; but you will probably encounter some of them in your travels through the wild parts of California.

Badgers

TO SEE THEM... look in remote grasslands and arid regions.

These small yellow-gray mammals have more power than their 12 to 20 pounds would indicate. These nocturnal creatures are identified by short, powerful legs, a small bush tail, short rounded ears, and a generally flattened appearance. They have a keen sense of smell that helps them locate eggs and burrowing rodents. The young are born in April and May.

Beavers

TO SEE THEM... they are found mainly in the northeastern part of the state, along streams, rivers, and lakes.

These are the most interesting and industrious of rodents. They are famous for their dams built of sticks, rocks, tree trunks, mud, and anything else available. The resulting ponds are used to protect their homes, called lodges, which are made of sticks and mud. Beavers living along deep rivers burrow dens into river banks. Breaks in levees in the Sacramento River delta are sometimes blamed on these burrowing beavers.

The largest North American rodents, beavers weigh 30 to 40 pounds and are characterized by flat, wide tails, and large webbed feet. The tails are sometimes slapped on the water as warnings to other beavers against territorial intrusion. They feed at night on twigs and bark of riperian trees, roots, and grasses. Beavers are monogamous, breeding in February, and bearing young in April and May.

Black Bears
TO SEE THEM... they are found in many forested, mountainous areas, and are most easily seen in parks and other protected places.

Black bears are most often encountered as nuisances in national parks, and other mountain areas, where they have learned that people are an easy source of food. These bears actually come in a variety of colors: black, brown and blond. Usually weighing between 200 and 400 pounds, they walk with a plodding, almost clumsy gait; but can move fast when motivated. Bears have a keen sense of smell, but poor vision. Their noses take them to their omnivorous diet of berries, seeds, roots, leaves, and other vegetation. Most of the meat they consume is carrion. They have no natural enemies.

Twin cubs are usually born to sows during their dormant winter period, though one or three young are not uncommon. The education she gives her cubs in bear skills usually takes a year.

Bobcats
TO SEE THEM... look in grassy and brushy areas throughout the wild parts of the state.

Upon first glance you might think this is just a big house cat. But then you will notice the spots, the bobbed tail, and the tufted ears. Bobcats are usually nocturnal, but are sometimes seen during the day. These 15 to 40 pound cats have excellent eyesight for stalking at night, usually feeding on mice, gophers, chipmunks, squirrels, rabbits, and other small prey. Kittens are born in April and May.

Burros
TO SEE THEM... they live in arid and semi-arid parts of the state.

Burros are the largest and most maligned desert animals. A ban-

Bobcats avoid people, and are usually seen as fleeting glimpses. Their numbers are declining due to increased trapping for their fur.

doned by prospectors in the last century, they have not only survived, they have thrived in some of the most inhospitable places, despite efforts to eradicate them. They are accused of denuding rangeland, polluting watering holes, and threatening the survival of desert bighorns. In Death Valley National Monument their numbers are being controlled by a live-trap adoption program which the park department hopes will result in the elimination of burros from the monument by the late 1980's.

Coyotes

TO SEE THEM... they are common in mountains, forests, deserts, brushland, and even up to the outskirts of many California cities.

Coyotes are the most common predatory mammal in the state. They are seen roaming the countryside day or night, but are more often heard than seen. Their soulful serenades usually start with a few short barks, followed by long howls, with yips, barks, and extra howls added.

Coyotes are California's largest native dog, weighing about 20 to 40 pounds. They have long legs, a long bushy tail, and shaggy fur. Blamed for killing livestock, they have survived, and even thrived, in the face of a hundred year effort to exterminate them. But it is exceptional for coyotes to eat domestic animals, their normal prey being rodents and other small animals, as well as seeds and berries. Keen hearing, excellent sense of smell, and sharp vision and intelligence make them effective hunters. Coyotes breed from mid-January to early March, and about six pups are usually born between March and May. Families live in dens usually in rocky places with underbrush.

Coyotes are a symbol of the west as much for their indomitable spirit as for their hauntingly beautiful yips and howls. Man's war against these clever canines is backfiring by killing off the weakest and least intelligent individuals and leaving the cleverest and strongest to carry on the species.

San Joaquin kit foxes have small bodies and exceptionally large ears. They are capable of sudden bursts of speed in pursuit of game.

Foxes

TO SEE THEM... see below.

These small, slender canines are easily identified by their sharp, pointed faces, large ears, and bushy tails. Their diet includes rodents, eggs, and carrion. Here are the three species of fox you might see in California:

RED FOX: This species has a yellow-red coat and weighs up to 12 pounds. They live in the open country and forests of the Sacramento Valley and the Sierra.

GRAY FOX: Our most common fox, they live in low mountain areas, usually between 1,000 and 3,000 feet, in chaparral, forests, and rocky terrain. They weigh between seven and 13 pounds.

KIT FOX: These are the smallest foxes, weighing only three to five pounds. They are identified by small, slender bodies and exceptionally large ears. They feed on rodents and live in arid and semi-arid country.

Marmots

TO SEE THEM... they live near and above timberline in high mountains.

These large rodents are the acquaintance of backpackers and mountaineers who venture high in the Sierra and other high ranges. Marmots only weigh five to ten pounds, though their thick yellow-brown fur and stocky bodies make them seem larger than they really are. They are often seen sunning themselves on rocks near high mountain meadows, where they eat prodigious amounts of grass, leaves, and other vegetation. It takes a lot of eating in summer to build up enough fat to last through the long alpine winters.

Minks
TO SEE THEM.. they live near streams in the northern Sierra and northern coastal ranges.

These aquatic carnivores have long, slender bodies, short legs, and dense, dark-brown fur. They are usually nocturnal, and rarely seen. They eat mice, crayfish, frogs, rabbits, and other small prey. Minks live solitary lives, except during the breeding season between February and March.

Mountain Lions
TO SEE THEM... look in rugged mountain and forest areas.

The sight of mountain lions in the wild is exciting and rare. Concealed by their tawny-gray colors, these great cats move silently and nearly indiscernibly through the landscape, avoiding people like the plague. Though you will probably never see a lion in the wild, you are very likely to see their tracks, especially in muddy places. They weigh 90 to 180 pounds when mature, and feed mainly on deer.

Mother lions usually choose caves in rocky places for their dens. Two or three kittens are usually born in spring, though they may arrive at any time of year. Kittens start out life with yellow-brown coats with black spots; but by the time they are a year old they turn gray-brown or red-brown like their parents.

Mule Deer
TO SEE THEM... they are common throughout most of the state.

Named for their large mule-like ears, these graceful herbivores

are always on the alert against predators, mainly humans and mountain lions. Also called blacktailed deer, they rely on speed for their main defense, although their hooves can also be formidable weapons. They eat mainly twigs, leaves, buds, and grasses. They are easily identified by their large ears, white rumps, and black tails.

Fawns are born in spring, often in pairs and triplets, and are camouflaged with reddish-brown coats and white spots. Antlers, grown by bucks in spring, are shed in winter.

Opossums
TO SEE THEM... look in woodlands and along streams.

North America's only marsupials, opossums are common through most of the state. Though abundant, their nocturnal habits make them hard to find. They have gray fur, long narrow faces, and grow to the size of a large house cat Their secret of survival is a high birth rate and a broad diet. Females begin breeding at six months and may bear as many as 18 young, which are as small as bees and live in their mothers' pouches for 65 days. Females usually give birth to one litter each year.

Pronghorn Antelopes
TO SEE THEM... they live in the open prairies and sagebrush plains of the northeastern part of the state.

Reaching speeds up to 60 miles per hour, pronghorns are one of the fastest land animals in the world. These graceful speedsters once roamed most of California; but now live in the wild only in parts of Modoc, Lassen, Plumas, and Inyo counties. They are most plentiful in Modoc County.

Pronghorns are not really antelopes at all, but the sole remaining species of a family called antilocapridae. They are distinguished

by reddish-tan coats, white rumps, and curved horns, each with prongs projecting forward. Bucks form harems of seven or eight does, which breed in September and October, and bear young in spring. They migrate between summer and winter feeding grounds, where they eat grasses, leaves, and sagebrush.

Raccoons

TO SEE THEM... they live nearly everywhere, but prefer wooded areas near streams and lakes.

These are one of California's most common wild mammals, at home nearly everywhere, even in cities. They are characterized by long, yellowish-gray fur, black masklike markings across their eyes, and long, black-ringed tails. Their hand-like front feet are extremely manipulative, leaving easily identifiable tracks that resemble tiny human hand prints. Raccoons are omnivores, eating nearly anything they can get their hands on. They wander far in search of food, though they usually live near water, which is used for washing food when possible. Breeding is done in February and March, and females bear young in April and May.

Ring-Tailed Cats

TO SEE THEM... look near streams in rocky canyons below 6,000

feet.

Someone once described these small predators as having the bodies of squirrels, the front feet of cats, and the tails of raccoons. They weigh only three pounds and are characterized by large ears and eyes, light brown-gray fur, and bushy tails that are nearly as long as their bodies. These cats are nocturnal, and rarely seen; but when they are it is often in pairs. They eat mainly birds, fruit, rats, mice, and other rodents. Young are born in May and June.

River Otters

TO SEE THEM... they live in woodlands along streams and near lakes in the northern part of the state and in the Sierra.

These playful little fellows are fun to watch, but are rarely seen because they avoid people. River otters have long, slender bodies that weigh about 20 pounds. Their webbed feet and long tails make them maneuverable enough to catch fish, as well as aquatic insects and frogs. Otters mate in summer, and two to four young are born to a litter the following spring.

Skunks

TO SEE THEM... they are found in brushlands and sparsely wooded areas throughout the state.

There are two species of skunks in California: striped and spotted. Both are omnivores, eating insects, rodents, berries, fruits, and many other plants and small animals. SPOTTED SKUNKS weigh only one to two pounds and are identified by black bodies with broken white stripes on their necks, backs, and sides. STRIPED SKUNKS weigh six to 14 pounds and have black bodies with V-shaped white stripes on their backs.

Weasels

TO SEE THEM... look in brushy areas and open woodlands near water.

These long, slender carnivores change colors, from reddish-brown in summer to white in winter where there is snow. Weighing less than a pound, they feed on rabbits, mice, chipmunks, and other small prey. Their young are born in the spring. California has two species of weasels: LONG-TAILED WEASELS: the larger and more common of the two, being seen in most of the state. SHORT-

TAILED WEASELS: found in northwestern California and at high elevations in the Sierra as far south as Yosemite.

Wolverines

TO SEE THEM... they live in remote parts of the Sierra near timberline.

The largest members of the weasel family, wolverines are identified by short, powerful legs, small eyes, and dense, dark-brown fur. When mature they weigh 20 to 45 pounds and are about 3 feet long. These solitary hunters eat mice, gophers, porcupines, and marmots. Females bear young once every two to three years. They are seen almost exclusively in wilderness.

Mammal watching in California's deserts requires more than just a love for wildlife. It also requires the inner-discipline to get up before dawn and the patience to wait quietly at a waterhole. Desert mammals such as foxes, coyotes, and ring-tailed cats sleep away the heat of day, becoming active only when the sun has gone down. Since these animals need water, they can be seen near water holes and springs, which can be identified on U.S. Geological Survey topographic maps, and by calling the Federal Bureau of Land Management offices. Sit quietly and patiently near the water, but not at the water's edge, about an hour before dawn.

Tracks:

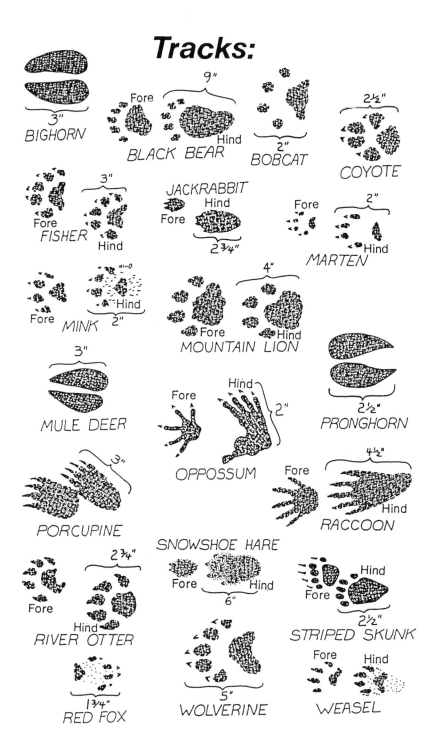

BIGHORN 3"

BLACK BEAR
Fore
Hind
9"

BOBCAT 2"

COYOTE 2½"

FISHER
Fore
Hind
3"

JACKRABBIT
Fore
Hind
2¾"

MARTEN
Fore
Hind
2"

MINK
Fore
Hind
2"

MOUNTAIN LION
Fore
Hind
4"

MULE DEER 3"

OPPOSSUM
Fore
Hind
2"

PRONGHORN 2½"

PORCUPINE 3"

RACCOON
Fore
Hind
4½"

SNOWSHOE HARE
Fore
Hind
6"

RIVER OTTER
Fore
Hind
2¾"

STRIPED SKUNK
Fore
Hind
2½"

RED FOX 1¾"

WOLVERINE 5"

WEASEL
Fore
Hind

Location Index: